SIGN & SYMBOL COMMUNICATION FOR MENTALLY HANDICAPPED PEOPLE

Philip R. Jones and Ailsa Cregan

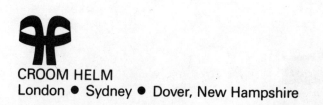

CROOM HELM

London • Sydney • Dover, New Hampshire

© 1986 Philip R. Jones and Ailsa Cregan
Illustrations by Tracey Asbery and Ailsa Cregan
Croom Helm Ltd, Provident House, Burrell Row,
Beckenham, Kent BR3 1AT

Croom Helm Australia Pty Ltd, Suite 4, 6th Floor,
64-76 Kippax Street, Surry Hills, NSW 2010, Australia

British Library Cataloguing in Publication Data
Jones, Philip R.
  Signs and symbols: communication for
  mentally handicapped people.
  1. Mentally handicapped—Education
  2. Communication—Study and teaching
  I. Title   II. Cregan, Ailsa
  371.92′8   LC4815

  ISBN 0-7099-1431-8
  ISBN 0-7099-1479-2 Pbk

Croom Helm, 51 Washington Street, Dover,
New Hampshire, 03820, USA

Library of Congress Cataloging in Publication Data
Jones, Philip R., 1952–
  Signs and symbols.

  Bibliography: p.
  Includes index.
    1. Mentally handicapped—means of communication.
  2. Nonverbal communication. I. Cregan, Ailsa,
  1938–   . II. Title.
  HV3004.5.J66   1986   419   85-31348
  ISBN 0-7099-1431-8
  ISBN 0-7099-1479-2 (pbk.)

Phototypeset by Words & Pictures Ltd,
Thornton Heath, Surrey
Printed and bound in Great Britain
by Billing & Sons Limited, Worcester.

CONTENTS

LIST OF FIGURES AND TABLES

Figures

Tables

ABOUT THE AUTHORS

Phil Jones started his academic career obtaining an honours degree in Zoology at the University of London before training as a teacher at Goldsmiths College of the same University. Later he achieved an M.Sc. in Experimental Psychology at the University of Sussex and then taught for several years in primary, secondary and special schools. During this time he studied for a Certificate in Educational Research at the Open University. Subsequently at the Child Development Research Unit, University of Nottingham he trained professionally as an Educational Psychologist achieving an M.A. degree.

For several years he worked as a psychologist to the Spastics Society where an interest developed in non-speech alternatives for the handicapped. Currently he has a post as an Educational Psychologist in Nottinghamshire, assisting in the development of initiatives as disparate as hypnosis and family therapy. Additionally he is engaged in research investigating special reading techniques for the developmentally young.

Phil Jones has published on a wide range of topics in scientific and professional journals and maintains a continuous interest in the social and political welfare of intellectually disabled people.

Ailsa Cregan pursued her interest in language and literature by studying English at Edinburgh University, where she obtained an M.A. Honours degree. She then taught English for some time at secondary modern and grammar schools.

For nine years she was a housewife. During this period, she assisted in setting up a nursery school, became a voluntary tutor in the Adult Literacy Scheme and acted as home teacher to a school phobic boy.

On her return to school-attached teaching — precipitated by the financial needs of her family and playwright husband — she had her first real taste of Special Education as a teacher of multiply handicapped children on the ward of a subnormality hospital. Subsequent posts have all been in the field of Special Education, mainly in schools for children who are severely mentally handicapped. She is now headteacher of such a school in the London Borough of Brent.

While teaching full time, she studied through the Cambridge Institute of Education to obtain an Advanced Diploma in the Education of Children with Special Needs. The subject of her diploma Long Study was 'Sigsymbols', the non-speech system she was developing in the course of its classroom use. This has led to the publication of a Sigsymbol teaching pack as well as a broader concern and involvement in solving practical problems of communication at all intellectual levels.

ACKNOWLEDGEMENTS

Over a number of years, many people have directly or indirectly influenced the shape of this book. The authors are, however, particularly grateful to the following for their specific and helpful suggestions: Patricia Bailey, David Cregan, Bob Denman, Jim Ferrer, Bill Gillham, Philip Gore, Marguerette Green, Tim Hardwick, Janet Hulme, Victoria Jenkins, Pat Jones, Kate Kirk, Miranda Llewellyn-Jones, Professor Lyle L. Lloyd, Mick Lock, Andy and Ruth Lowe, Sheila Menon, Jeff Millar, Elizabeth Newson, Adrian Searle, Jenni Smith, Carol Stanton, Brian Stratford, Lorna Szyszczak, Sue Thurman, Sue White and Deryk Wilson.

Some of the illustrations are based on artistic ideas which were discussed with Allan Bell, Adrian Rudd and Allan Blain, to whom the authors also express their thanks.

The authors and publishers wish to thank the Royal National Institute for the Deaf and Gallaudet College Press for permission to reproduce illustrations from the British Standard Manual Alphabet and the American Manual Alphabet respectively. Similarly they thank the Blissymbolics Communication Institute for permission to use copyright Blissymbols.

They also acknowledge with gratitude their debt to all the sign and symbol systems and their proponents or originators who through demonstration, text or personal contact made a contribution to the written and illustrated form of this book.

PREFACE

For a variety of motor, neurological or sensory reasons, some children have great problems in developing speech while other children and some adults either lose the power of speech or have difficulty in using it. Temporarily or permanently, they need an alternative form of communication.

Severely mentally handicapped people, some with additional disabilities, may also require an alternative support or supplement to speech. The communication needs of this group, in so far as they can be met by non-speech systems, are the primary concern of this book.

Articles and workshops on this topic have customarily promoted specific ideas or systems, or reviewed or researched methodological issues from an academic standpoint. The present publication is an attempt to bridge the gap between the two approaches. It is hoped that this straightforward presentation of the subject will stimulate readers to widen their knowledge of the application of sign and symbol systems used for communication purposes. Besides providing basic information on a range of non-speech systems used for communication purposes, the book contains numerous practical suggestions on ways in which mentally handicapped people may be helped by using them.

The book is intended to be of use to a wide range of professionals, as well as to families and friends of mentally handicapped people. Readers may also include staff in Education, Health and the Social Services whose knowledge of non-speech systems is limited or whose experience is very specific. Those who wish to pursue further particular topics that are introduced here will be helped by the annotated bibliography in Appendix A, the sources of further information listed in Appendix B and the references in the text. Technological aids and their suppliers are listed and briefly described in Appendix C.

Illustrations of manual signs are intended only as examples rather than for precise use as a reference. Signing in any case should be learned from a qualified instructor. Proponents of some symbol systems also prefer teachers to undergo a relevant course of instruction.

The book largely reflects the United Kingdom scene, both in its background and the choice of systems described. However, many of the points that are made, the discussion of issues, technological aids and teaching approaches, are universally applicable.

A Note on Gender

While obviously professionals and all involved in the care and education of mentally handicapped people may be of either sex, in the following text they are consistently referred to as female to avoid the cumbersome use of 'he or she'. Again for stylistic reasons, to make differentiation simpler, mentally handicapped clients are therefore spoken of as male, except of course when a reference is made to a particular female client.

INTRODUCTION

The influences that lead to a particular outcome, perhaps in a way that was never originally envisaged, may only become clear with hindsight. So it is with the current use of communication systems other than speech for helping mentally handicapped people. Among the influences contributing to the present situation in the United Kingdom the following may be identified: a growing awareness of the needs and rights of handicapped people; some (even if still not enough) enlightened legislation of the 1970s and early 1980s; a new philosophy of learning and behaviour; and widespread interest in the nature of language.

Growing Awareness

In 1968, the groundswell of opinion in many countries resulted in the United Nations Declaration of the General and Special Rights of the Mentally Handicapped, which formally asserted that 'the mentally retarded person has . . . the same rights as other human beings'. His rights included 'such education . . . as will enable him to develop his ability and maximum potential'; in addition, where possible he should 'live with his own family . . . and participate in different forms of community life . . . If care in an institution becomes necessary it should be provided in surroundings and other circumstances as close as possible to those of normal life'.

During the 1960s, various organisations in the UK had been pressing for a better deal for mentally handicapped children and adolescents. In response to their challenge that the educational system was failing to meet special needs the Scott Committee was set up. Its brief was to consider the training of the then mainly unqualified staff in training centres run by Local Health Authorities and schools attached to subnormality hospitals, both of which catered for children who were considered to be ineducable in mainstream schools. The committee's report (1962) recommended that staff should receive a two-year course of training to equip them to provide education, and not merely occupation, for their mentally handicapped charges. Although legislation did not follow, more positive attitudes were being reflected in the contemporary theory of 'normalisation'; this urged that handicapped people should be denied none of the rights available to other citizens, especially those which would help them lead a normal life.

Professional interest of the time was sufficient for annual conferences to be

1

held on the subject of 'research relevant to the education of backward children'. At one of these conferences, the then Secretary of State for Education and Science expressed his concern that in the best interest of individual children there should be multi-disciplinary co-operation between the professions. Only a few years later came legislation for multi-disciplinary liaison between services to mentally handicapped children.

Legislation

The year 1961 in the United States saw the setting up of President Kennedy's Panel on Mental Retardation, whose reporting back stimulated many practical public initiatives. In the UK not until 1970 did pressure from many sources lead to the Education (Handicapped Children) Act being passed, which took the step of transferring responsibility for educating severely mentally handicapped children from the local Health Authorities to the Education Authorities.

From then on, these children were no longer officially designated a medical problem. They became entitled to the full range of professional educational services from Education Authority advisers, welfare officers, educational psychologists and qualified teachers.

Although the act set in motion changes with far-reaching implications, predictably the changes did not occur overnight. For example, in the early days, a teacher – even a headteacher – in a special school for severely mentally handicapped children required only minimal qualifications. Twenty-five years after the act, a specialised degree or higher diploma may be expected of anyone seeking a post of responsibility in such a school.

In 1971, in the wake of the Seebohm Report, the government legislated for a Central Training Council for Education and Training in Social Work whose purpose was to co-ordinate the work of the three different departments within local authorities delivering some form of social service for children. In the same year there also appeared a government White Paper entitled 'Better Services for the Mentally Handicapped', which aimed to improve hospital services and recommended a joint approach by the different agencies of Education, Health and the Social Services.

Children were better provided for than adults and indeed in relative terms the position is unchanged today. When a handicapped child grows up, parents face the less natural but even more onerous task of caring for the still-dependent adult. At the same time, less outside support may be available. The comment of one parent sums up the experience of many: 'When my daughter was young, you couldn't get them off the doorstep – every week, teachers, health visitors, physiotherapists and social workers. Now she's leaving school, nobody seems to want to know.' Despite the difficulties at home, however, to many parents the idea of placing their child of whatever age in a long-stay hospital runs wholly counter to their belief in the personal benefits of living at home in a 'normal' environment.

The Jay Report (1979), which stemmed from an inquiry into mental nursing and care, was fully in sympathy with such views, considering hospital residence undesirable. The need for handicapped people to remain in touch with the community was stressed, either through living at home with better support or in small residential units. The report recommended a non-medical approach by a new profession of carers who would be trained 'home-makers', trained to liaise closely with parents and also to help a mentally handicapped person's overall development – physical, emotional, educational and social. In other words, they were to pursue the broadly educational aims of an enlightened parent.

In the field of education, parallel aims received attention in the Warnock Report (1978), entitled 'Special Educational Needs'. Among its many recommendations, the report emphasised the importance of viewing the parents of mentally handicapped children as educational partners right from the start, and of educating children not according to a labelled category but in accordance with their individual special needs. Wherever practicable, integration was advocated between handicapped and non-handicapped children. Three years later, the Education Act (1981) legislated for many of Warnock's recommendations, giving approval in principal (if not always in practice) to the provision of fully adequate resources in schools which catered for children with special needs. These included schools for 'children with severe learning difficulties', the new official educational description of severely mentally handicapped children.

A New Philosophy in Education

Educational approaches in special schools have changed over the years, though the importance of social learning has always been acknowledged. In the 1970s a developmental philosophy was prevalent, equating mental age with chronological age. Thus for a child with a mental age of three to five years nursery school methods were considered quite appropriate. Within a stimulating environment, children were encouraged to play freely, their activities centring mainly on tactile and three-dimensional materials. It was anticipated that this kind of experience would enable them to learn by discovery, picking up skills incidentally in the course of their play.

However, no matter how rich or stimulating the environment, the anticipated skills were rarely acquired, whether these were conceptual or practical. It became clear that for handicapped children the learning-by-discovery approach had its limitations.

In the USA, learning problems were being addressed by psychologists familiar with Skinner's philosophy of behaviourism (Skinner 1938, 1953 and

1969). This will now be outlined, with the technical terms italicised. According to this philosophy, the way people behave is contingent upon what goes on around them: they learn the *behaviours* that are *reinforced* by their *consequences*. *Positive reinforcement* (which the learner must experience as a reward) will help to establish a new behaviour; *negative reinforcement* (which may be actual punishment, or may merely be withholding or withdrawal of positive reinforcement) will *extinguish* an existing behaviour.

Behavioural techniques provide a structured framework for learning. First, blocks to learning can be removed by extinguishing undesirable behaviours. Then, after an objective has been decided upon, it is broken down into a series of incremental steps that can be described in terms of the learner's behaviour. This process, known as *task analysis*, helps to determine step-by-step *teaching goals*, closely enough sequenced to suit the child's (or adult's) learning ability. Since the goals are specific *observable behaviours*, the learner's success in achieving them can be precisely assessed.

During teaching sessions, while a new behaviour is being established, a *schedule of continuous reinforcement* (i.e. rewarding every single correct response) is the most effective, but when maintaining an established behaviour it is desirable to *fade* this to intermittent reinforcement. A teacher can *shape* the learner's responses in the direction of the *target behaviour* by physically *prompting* him to make the correct response so that his learning is *errorless*; once learning has taken place, prompts can be faded. A running assessment of progress is essential to enable goals and teaching methods to be modified if necessary; assessment is facilitated by precise recording, which is an integral part of the behavioural technique.

(For further reading, see *Behaviour Modification* (Wilcock 1978) for a brief account, or *Behaviour Modification for the Mentally Handicapped* (Yule and Carr 1980) for a fuller series of readings. Practical applications of behaviour modification can be found in *Analysis of Programmes for Teaching* (Kiernan 1981) and a breakdown of a behavioural programme appears in Chapter 5 of this book.)

For children who were not apparently benefiting from the discovery approach, structured learning of a sequence of skills was an alternative that offered encouraging possibilities. Though the technique provided no ready-made rationale for choosing and analysing objectives, Skinner himself had turned his attention to language (Skinner 1957) and American psychologists went on to devise several initial language programmes, structured on the behavioural model, such as the Distar, Peabody and Goal Language Kits. (Brief accounts of each of these can be found in *Ways and Means* (Tebbs 1978). Originally intended for use with disadvantaged pre-school children in the USA, they were exported to other countries and also came to be used with mentally handicapped children at home and abroad.

Special school curricula already incorporated social learning as an aspect of education which merited special attention. Relevant to this, and of even greater specific interest to many professionals from post-war times to the present day, was the whole topic of language and communication.

Language and Communication

In a human being, communication difficulties are arguably the most significant deficit of all. If acute, not only do they exclude him from any major involvement in our society, but also they may limit intellectual development and will certainly hinder educational progress. Mental handicap always impairs language and communication to some degree and – broadly speaking – the more severe the handicap the greater the impairment. When mentally handicapped people attempt and fail to communicate, they may express their frustration through anti-social behaviour or resort to socially unacceptable ways of gaining attention.

Practical aspects of communication are the special province of speech therapists and speech-language clinicians – to use respectively the British and American terms. The latter gives a clearer picture of their role in relation to mentally handicapped people, but, though the Quirk Report (1972) on speech therapy in the UK fully acknowledges the wider role, it retains the designation 'speech therapist'. Speech therapists aim to develop functional communication in their clients, whatever the most effective means of expression and understanding may be.

Among the clientele of speech therapists are people with impaired hearing, including the profoundly deaf, for whom a more natural form of communication than speech is manual signing – the language that has evolved naturally within the deaf community. Despite the effectiveness of signing for this population, until recently it was almost always rejected by speech therapists and teachers working in schools for the hearing impaired, as they feared that its use would discourage speech. It was denigrated as not being a 'true' language, in disregard of the more relevant point that it was functional.

In fact anxieties that signing may hold back speech are not based on evidence (Stokoe 1976). On the contrary, profoundly deaf children who have never learned to communicate by signing have even greater difficulty in learning speech than those who acquire it as a second language to signing. Fortunately, as times have changed, so in many quarters has the second-class image of signing; nowadays the deaf are no longer alone in upholding the integrity and effectiveness of signing as equal to that of conventional languages, though different in medium. Replacing the oralist (speech only) philosophy in many schools for the deaf is the philosophy of Total Communication, whereby anything and everything which helps to convey the intended message is encouraged, including 'gestures, postures, facial expressions, tones of voice, formal speech and non-speech systems and simultaneous communication' (Kopchick and Lloyd 1976). Obviously a non-speech system of signing has a contribution to make to Total Communication.

In the early 1970s, in the north of England, signing was introduced to deaf children who were also mentally handicapped. Soon afterwards, research began into the potential of signing for non-deaf mentally handicapped hospital residents and, at first mainly through the good offices of speech therapists, its use spread to other schools and establishments for mentally handicapped people. Happily for all concerned, the new behavioural techniques were also gaining currency and were well suited to the teaching of signing.

Over the same period, the wider interest in language and communication continued among psychologists, linguists, philosophers and biologists. All were fascinated by what was supposed to be a feature unique to mankind – though the view of its uniqueness was challeneged by some research with primates (Gardner and Gardner 1069; Premack and Premack 1972). This indicated that oral speech made demands on physical, neurological and mental development that could by bypassed by translating language into a visual mode, which was a discovery with vital practical implications for any non-speaking population. The Gardners investigated the potential of natural gesture as a means of communication, and also, by extension, non-representational manual signs; the Premacks experimented with word-symbols in the form of abstract plastic shapes.

Following the Premacks' findings, other researchers used similar manipulable plastic word-symbols with severely mentally handicapped children, achieving encouraging results. Exploratory work was also undertaken using non-alphabetic graphic (written) word-symbols to assist children with severe physical handicaps to communicate. As with the structured language programmes, these and several other non-speech communication alternatives not originally conceived for this purpose came to be used for the benefit of mentally handicapped people.

Non-speech Systems

The right of mentally handicapped people to lead as far as possible a normal life has been officially recognised, and for normality communication is essential. Since many of these people are not able to acquire speech naturally, if at all they need trained personnel to teach them some means of communication, and integrated services so that whatever their day and residential setting the best use is made of opportunities for learning. Legislation in the UK over the past two decades has, in part at least, made it possible to meet these needs. In addition, the advent of behavioural techniques into education, suitable for the teaching of a non-speech system, has paved the way for more widespread use of such systems.

Their use has indeed mushroomed within services for mentally handicapped people, so that those with responsibility for selecting a system are faced with a bewildering choice. This is made no easier by the fact that, in this context at least, most of the systems are relatively new and unproven. Proponents of one system may promote it zealously, ignoring areas of uncertainty, while critics highlight limitations and challenge the pet ideas of innovators. In fact, few of the strongly held ideas are backed up by research. Every option has something to offer and the task is to select the system to suit the situation.

This book, as part of its underlying aim to help mentally handicapped people to communicate, seeks to equip readers with a basic knowledge of a number of non-speech systems, their background, rationale and characteristics. References in the text and suggestions for further reading offer those requiring it a more comprehensive account of particular systems or related topics.

The systems divide into two main types. Manual signing systems are described and discussed in Chapter 2; for the sake of convenience, manual signs will be referred to simply as 'signs'. Chapter 3 deals with two other types of word-symbol mentioned in the introduction, i.e. manipulable symbol-shapes and graphic (written or drawn) symbols; at times, these will be referred to simply as 'symbols'.

The rest of the book presents information as follows: Chapter 1 discusses the acceptability of non-speech alternatives to the people involved in introducing them to clients. It also considers a variety of clients who might benefit from their use and looks at some methods of assessing clients. Once Chapters 2 and 3 have acquainted readers with specific sign and symbol systems, Chapter 4 reviews some of the available display methods and technical aids to help clients with additional physical handicaps. Some possible teaching approaches are suggested in Chapter 5. Chapter 6, in attempting to sum up, makes general comparisons between sign and symbol systems and considers different potential users and different teaching settings. Finally, we take a brief look at possible areas for research in the future.

1 USING A NON-SPEECH SYSTEM: WHO CAN BE HELPED AND HOW?

Mentally handicapped people share the universal need to communicate. At a time when research has shown that non-speech systems can be an effective way of doing this when speech is deficient, a new philosophy of behaviour has radically affected teaching methods. Legislation has provided the resources for, among other things, trained personnel to teach the communication skills that contribute so much to life in society.

However, not all of those who are closely concerned with mentally handicapped people find new ideas and methods easy to accept. They may yet have to discover, for example, that anything so familiar and 'normal' as speech might be usefully replaced or supplemented by a quite different communication vehicle. The present chapter begins by considering some of their problems in coming to terms with this – problems that must be overcome as the ground is prepared to introduce a non-speech system. It goes on to describe the characteristics of clients who may benefit. Finally it looks at some ways of assessing clients in order that teaching programmes may begin at the optimum level for each individual, building on existing competence and attempting to extend it.

Acceptance of a Non-speech System

'Normalisation' has been put forward as an important aspect of the education of mentally handicapped people, so that their differences from 'normal' society are minimised. Some might therefore query the wisdom of introducing an 'abnormal' non-speech system. Although possession of at least some form of communication is the essence of normality, families, professionals and many who work in establishments for mentally handicapped people may be reluctant to envisage alternatives to speech.

The Family

When a handicapped child is born or his handicap first revealed, parents and families naturally suffer shock. Often parents feel (quite unjustified) guilt or shame and become depressed about the future life of the child. Brothers and sisters may become resentful or jealous at the extra attention needed by their peer, and because he is 'different' be embarrassed to bring friends home or even to acknowledge the existence of this member of the family. All may feel an undefined hope that somehow the abnormality may be cured, rather in the manner of a medical ailment. In this climate, introducing an idiosyncratic communication system hardly appears as progress.

Some families may have adjusted well to the handicapped person in their midst. For them the problem of accepting a new system may be the threat to their accustomed way of life, as a previously passive individual learns to express himself and begins to make new demands upon them. Sometimes the handicapped child or adult learns to communicate with a professional in a way that was never possible within the family, so that parents feel alienated or robbed of a special relationship.

However, forewarned is forearmed, and if a teacher or therapist is prepared for possible resistance there is time to prepare genuinely helpful replies to allay fears. It can be pointed out that as parents become familiar and at ease with the system that the professional has introduced, they too will be able to use it, thus enriching their relationship with their child as they get to know him even better. The parental role is crucial in a child's communication development; at home, in a relaxed and loving atmosphere, the parents can provide opportunities for practising communication, when their child can be confident that any attempts he may make to communicate will be attended to and reciprocated.

Sympathetic discussions can alter perceptions. The changes which accompany newly expressed demands may be a threat from one point of view. From another, and for the handicapped person, they are an exciting step forward which could greatly enhance his quality of life. Someone who is making sense to those around him (whatever the means of communication) appears as a person in his own right. This deters the 'Does he take sugar?' approach – which is a denial of individual status – and encourages direct communication. Families can be reassured that their own responsiveness will stimulate and extend the communication of their handicapped member.

A family's resistance to signing may diminish with the knowledge that it is used by the intellectually normal deaf community. They may have the opportunity of watching highly intelligent deaf people signing, or signing and speaking, on television programmes. Possible difficulties in learning signs can be reduced if the professional working with the family provides illustrations of, at the very least, a core vocabulary of signs and is willing to supply more on demand. One or more non-handicapped members of the family should be given basic tuition in signing.

If symbols are the chosen type of system, it is important for a family's involvement that a complete and up-to-date set is kept in the home and that family members are acquainted with strategies for using the symbols. If the equivalent word is written on or alongside each symbol, no-one need experience decoding problems and using symbols becomes reassuringly similar to the 'normal' reading process. A symbol system may be especially convenient for families whose first language is not English, for conventionally written words in both their own language and English can appear beside the symbols.

The Professionals

Personnel from numerous professions currently work in the field of mental handicap: teachers, speech therapists, occupational therapists, psychologists, educational advisers, social workers, administrators and others, both practitioners and researchers. In addition, since mentally handicapped people have a relatively high incidence of illness or conditions requiring medical attention, many health professionals are involved at some level, including psychiatrists, physicians, surgeons, nurses and physiotherapists. Although legislation has aimed to co-ordinate services, this range of professionals, through training and experience, brings an equally wide range of perspectives on working practice and attitudes: To these are added the views of untrained staff in residential, educational, training and industrial establishments, who are also in close and regular contact with a mentally handicapped clientele. New approaches to a communication programme need to harmonise this rich diversity.

Within any establishment, an innovator who wishes to set up the use of a non-speech system for the clientele is at an advantage if she has consulted with staff at all levels. A decision at management level in an establishment or department can be little more than theoretical unless staff in regular contact with clients give practical support. They are the ones who have to assimilate the system into their daily routine and there is a limit to what can be imposed from above without causing resentment. If the staff working at ground level can participate in the decisions which will affect them, then the associated project stands a better chance of engaging their goodwill.

Professionals lower down the ladder may face different difficulties in getting the use of a system accepted. When initiating a new project they need approval from those in charge and, ideally, active support. Their superiors, however, may be hard to convince that such an innovation will be advantageous or wise. Spelling out the potential practical benefits may help to persuade, mentioning, for example, the greater independence of clients who can express themselves and improved inter-communication between them and the staff. The innovator should also have in mind concrete proposals on the training of staff and clients. And at every stage, diplomacy and the provision of clear information are more likely to convince than an evangelical approach.

It is not helpful either to gloss over possible problems or to pretend they do not exist. For example, attitudes prevailing among the staff may have bearing on the type of system that can feasibly be introduced. A signing system will not only require preparation and practice, but also a real psychological (and physical) adjustment before it becomes habitual rather than intermittent, natural rather than embarrassingly self-conscious. Though, on the other hand, symbols need not be learned by heart, being an 'aided' system they are less portable than the 'unaided' systems of signing. Aid they may be, but still their means of display is an unavoidable encumbrance to be coped with by those caring for the client, whose attitude will be more positive if they can appreciate the advantages.

The Establishment

Few would dispute that establishments should be run for the benefit of their clients and that staff have a central part to play in pursuit of this aim. Ideally, in their work with mentally handicapped people, both professionals and non-professionals should contribute to programme planning for their clients, basing social and educational targets on the needs they have observed, developing clients' skills to meet present and future situations. Regular in-service training should keep staff up-to-date with current theory and practice. A progressive-thinking establishment will not be carried away by every fashionable trend, but thoughtful innovations will be well supported.

Inevitably, human nature and many establishments fall short of the ideal. Personal convenience may distract from the acknowledged aim of serving the clients. It is difficult, too, to avoid problems of liaison, especially in larger establishments such as long-stay hospitals which continue to be 'home' to many mentally handicapped people and which are served by multiple personnel. In such environments, even the most dedicated individual would find it well nigh impossible to involve every member of staff in a new venture, such as the implementation of a non-speech system. However, timetabling a comprehensive introduction for those who are directly concerned in one part of the venture (in, say, a ward or section) may still be a difficult task but not an impossible one. One or more day-long workshops may help solve the problem, with personnel attending as and when they can if their full-time attendance is not possible. A workshop can provide information and elementary training, besides instilling confidence that the project can be made to work. It is also a way of bringing together the multi-disciplinary staff within an establishment, whose shared learning experience will increase their awareness of belonging to a team.

Not only in hospitals, but also within schools and other day and residential establishments, in-service training may have to be fitted into the working day. Nevertheless, it is worth occasionally disrupting the regular timetable or routine if, as a result, staff become more involved and committed in the longer term and so better able to motivate their clients.

In the case of signing, follow-up workshops or regular training sessions are particularly important in promoting fluency and general acceptance. The authors know one large residential school which ran a half-hour training session for all available staff at the beginning of each day. Of course at the outset such sessions may be wholly dependent on the presence of one particular trained person to conduct them, but, as time goes on and the number of trained personnel increases, organisation becomes easier.

Whether an establishment's client group is large or small, staff teamwork is an important source of motivation. The greater the involvement at any point in a programme – initial training of staff, ongoing in-service support, training of clients, providing organisational or financial backing – the better for the continuing health of the programme. Naturally, too, the *raison d'être* for the existence of a project must not be forgotten: clients need constant encouragement and opportunity to communicate, which can only be provided if the people around them are prepared to spend the necessary time and trouble.

Having spoken in favour of widespread involvement, we would go on to add a rider: if any individual, no matter how untrained or unsophisticated, enables a handicapped person to communicate in the simplest way, then that is a worthwhile achievement. One of the authors took an eighteen-year-old non-speaking boy to an art exhibition by mentally handicapped people. His rapturous expression as he suddenly recognised the picture of a butterfly and made the sign 'butterfly' to draw attention to it was unforgettable.

A small beginning may serve as a model for greater things and the commitment of one person may bring about results which convert the sceptics.

The Clients

In this section, clients will be considered in terms of their condition or medical diagnosis, subdividing the apparently homogeneous group of 'mentally handicapped people' we have been referring to so far. Of course, as all who know and work with them are well aware, whatever characteristics they have in common with each other, as individuals they cannot be neatly categorised. Each personality shines out as unique. Our categories are simply a convenient way of indicating recurrent problems.

Use of non-speech systems is not confined to mentally handicapped people. Among intellectually normal users are people who are deaf, physically handicapped, aphasic, mute, or have defective speech following an accident or stroke. Our concern here, however, is with people who are quite severely mentally handicapped, with or without associated handicaps. We do not intend to give an exhaustive description of the various conditions, but rather to highlight features that disturb language development. A description of the normal sequence of development can be found later in this chapter, at the beginning of the section entitled 'Assessing the Client'.

Developmental Delay

A frequent description of mentally handicapped children is 'developmentally delayed' – a catch-all term for overall intellectual development which is slower than normal and may never reach normal levels. The delay often extends to physical development, both of size and motor ability. Normal curiosity is usually absent and the child may be exceptionally passive – often rather too 'good' and quiet as a baby. A severely delayed child may show little awareness of what is going on around him, apparently feeling no urge to communicate pleasure or pain.

The term is rarely used to describe adults who were 'delayed' as children and have never caught up with normal development, even though their behaviour and needs continue to resemble those of much younger clients.

The priority is stimulation of all kinds, with the aim or arousing the child's sensory and personal awareness of people and things in his immediate environment. As his interest grows, so may a desire to communicate, which may also be encouraged by simple games like 'peep-bo', hand-clapping, hiding and suddenly producing sweets or brightly coloured toys, to promote looking, listening and other responses. Learning programmes broken down into very small steps can be carried out at home or at school; the Portage Scheme (see Wessex Revised Portage Language Checklist (White and Earl 1983)) offers a wealth of information on stages in language development and teaching strategies to help a child achieve the next stage.

Some developmentally delayed children gain an understanding of speech, even if only of key words in context; a non-speech system may help these children to express themselves. At times it may also assist more specific difficulties. For example, a child with a defect in sequential memory (i.e. a problem over getting words in the right order) may be helped by using movable symbols which can be physically arranged and do not 'disappear' like speech or signs. Sometimes auditory processing is defective; in other words, despite there being no actual hearing loss, the client cannot sort out the meaning of what he hears because of very specific damage that has occurred in his brain. As this is a difficulty related to speech, a non-speech system may both assist understanding and lend support to the building up of language the client can express himself.

Non-speech systems are not, of course, a panacea for all ills. To benefit from them, clients' mental and physical abilities must be equal to the demands of an initial programme, as will be discussed further in the section on assessment later in this chapter. The crucial factor of motivation will also be discussed.

(For further reading, see *Mental Handicap* (Kirman and Bicknell 1975), *Getting Through to your Handicapped Child* (Newson and Hipgrave 1982) and *Handicapping Conditions in Children* (Gillham 1986).)

Autism

The diagnosis and cause(s) of autism have been the subject of much debate, but there is general agreement that autism is rather a cluster of features than a specific condition. Some so-called autistic people show exceptional ability in certain restricted areas, but many others suffer from global (overall) mental handicap. Emotional and social development are stunted and even when improvements take place they often appear mechanical or 'unnatural'. Autistic people frequently resort to socially unacceptable patterns of stimulation. Language disturbance is very common but often unrelated to sensory or motor impairment. Sometimes quite advanced linguistic skills may be achieved, but fail to generalise, especially within a social context. For example, an autistic person may be able to sing in tune a grammatically complex song, using the correct words, but be unable to make a simple verbal request for food or drink.

Some of the suggested explanations for the delayed or odd language development of autistic people may make a non-speech system especially relevant. One possibility is that because of their over-selective attention they may note non-linguistic aspects of spoken words (e.g. pitch or rhythm) while ignoring aspects. The transitory nature of spoken words makes it even more difficult for them to focus on every aspect. Another difficulty experienced by autistic people is in cross-modal coding, i.e. interpreting what is seen, heard, etc. into any other form. For example, cross-modal coding is essential in order to understand that the words that a person hears with his ears are equivalent to the words he speaks with his mouth. Non-speech systems may be relevant because the form in which they are produced and observed does not change: a graphic symbol retains a constant visual form and a manual sign (whether performed by the mentally handicapped client or by another person) can be observed directly by the client in its original form.

Learning a non-speech system may combat some of the language difficulties of autistic people and may also bring about other positive outcomes. Creedon (1976) describes the decrease of anti-social behaviour and increase of appropriate behaviour during a successful classroom-based non-speech programme. The improvement may be partly accounted for by the release of frustration as communication becomes possible. Another possibility is that autistic people, who are often very upset by breaks in routine, may find security through being regularly involved in a structured scheme of work.

Since difficulties in generalising from one situation to another are common, special programmes to promote the habit of using any communication skill in a 'real life' context may further assist social development. One or two teaching suggestions to this end appear in Chapter 5.

(For further reading, see *Autistic Children: A Guide for Parents* (Wing 1980), and *Autistic Children: Teaching, Community and Research Approaches* (Furneux and Roberts 1977).

More technical information can be found in the *Journal of Autism and Childhood Schizophrenia.*)

Physical Handicap

People often confuse physical handicap with mental handicap, thinking that because someone is wheelchair-bound, has some physical deformity or moves in an odd way, he must therefore be mentally handicapped. In fact, although the two conditions may be associated, this is not automatically so. Nevertheless, many mentally handicapped people do also suffer some form of physical handicap, stemming from a variety of causes. Some of these may occur after a child has been born 'normal', as in the case of meningitis, encephalitis or a road traffic accident resulting in brain damage. Many other children are already affected by the handicapping condition when they are born.

The commonest congenital (i.e. from birth) physical handicap is cerebral palsy (often abbreviated to CP), especially the type classified as spasticity, in which the limbs are stiff but weak and the body is given to sudden muscular spasm. The pattern of limbs that are affected varies, but when both arms are involved mental handicap is usually present, and it may be present in any case. Disorders of vision and hearing are common.

Some physical disabilities, including CP, impair muscular control of the speech organs, for example the tongue, so that the ability to speak is limited, either mildly or severely. Nerves associated with speech may lack normal sensitivity. Abnormalities of the hard or soft palette may be present. Multiple or acute conditions may prevent speech altogether.

Severe interference, even with apparently simple movements like reaching and grasping, may also occur and may make the fine movements of signing out of the question. An affected person may need a mechanical or electronic aid to gain access to a symbol system. A number of aids and methods of using them are described in Chapter 4.

The degree and likely effect of a disability must be expertly assessed. A medical diagnosis may be obtainable from a neurologist. Where speech organs appear to be involved, speech therapists/language clinicians are also qualified to make an assessment and to follow it up with advice and practical help in initiating or improving communication. From an informed standpoint, decisions can then be made as to whether the emphasis should be on finding a supplement, support and facilitator of speech or on finding the best alternative.

(For further reading, see *Handling the Young Cerebral Palsied Child at Home* (Finnie 1974) and for a comprehensive account of a wide range of conditions, see *Physically Handicapped Children: A Medical Atlas for Teachers* (Bleck and Nagel 1982).)

Hearing Handicap

If hearing is at all severely impaired, speech will automatically suffer, because at least some parts of some words will be quite inaudible. Not only will the affected person be unable to hear properly what is being said to him, and thus will find it difficult to understand, but in addition when he attempts to speak himself he will have impaired feedback through his ears. This will make self-correction difficult and pronunciation will suffer.

When a child's speech is not developing normally, his level of hearing should always be thoroughly checked. Even when another cause of speech delay is apparent, such as physical handicap or global developmental delay, it is worth while confirming that the hearing is not involved. The authors have known mentally handicapped children of all ages immediately appear brighter and more interested in their suroundings when they have been fitted with a hearing aid. In one extreme case, a man aged 39, who had spent years as a 'mentally handicapped' resident in a subnormality hospital, was discovered to be profoundly deaf and – as far as could be established – intellectually normal.

An audiologist based in a hospital or visiting a clinic will be able to measure the degree of hearing loss and advise on suitable aids. These cannot fully compensate for a severe loss and so the acquisition of a non-speech system may be an important aid to communication. Hearing aids do, however, allow the maximum use to be made of residual hearing.

(For further reading, see *A Guide for Parents of Very Young Deaf Children* (Grossman, no date) and *The Hearing-impaired Child and the Family* (Nolan and Tucker 1981).)

Down's Syndrome

Down's Syndrome is a genetically caused condition and although it is not a physical handicap as such, it does have a number of associated physical features. Besides the characteristic shape of head and eyes, and short fingers, these include other features that are less immediately obvious. Relevant in the present context is quite frequent hearing loss, deficient tongue control and abnormal vocal organs. People with Down's Syndrome are prone to chest infections and colds, which may also have an adverse effect on their hearing, with results as described in the section on hearing handicap.

In addition to the physical features of Down's Syndrome, there is a degree of mental handicap, ranging from very mild to fairly severe. Both physical and intellectual factors are likely to impair speech, but fortunately, even if they cannot speak, people with Down's Syndrome can often understand much of what other people are saying. They are often talented imitators and their social adjustment may be near to normal. The combination of being able to understand language, to imitate and to adjust socially makes them excellent candidates for learning a sign system. They are often motivated to make spontaneous use of this and are sometimes so encouraged by the effectiveness of signed communication that they make more confident and effective attempts to speak.

Recent research into the ability of young Down's children to learn to read (Buckley 1984) suggests that this can be a 'way in' to speech for some. Lower-ability children may be similarly stimulated by learning to read a non-alphabetic symbol system.

(For further reading, see *Down's Syndrome: An Introduction for Parents* (Cunningham 1982) and *Current Approaches to Down's Syndrome* (Lane and Stratford 1985).)

The 'Cocktail Party Syndrome'

The term 'cocktail party syndrome' is not a medical diagnosis of a condition, but is nevertheless quite widely used. It described the misleading fluency of some mentally handicapped clients who have developed reasonably good grammatical form and appear to make good contact with a listener. However, the 'chatter' flows on and on and out of control. The actual content of what is said is irrelevant or not appropriate to the context, and it forms little foundation for any but the most superficial interaction.

Mentally handicapped people who exhibit the cocktail party syndrome are frequently – though not exclusively – sufferers from hydrocephaly. This is a condition where too much fluid gathers within the brain causing pressure and, if it is not relieved, damage to the brain. The condition can be treated, but damage is not always prevented. Even when treatment is successful, the affected person is often of a talkative disposition.

One approach to modifying the cocktail party syndrome is to reduce the amount of language used so that the speaker is better able to think through what he is saying. If the vehicle for communication is less familiar, then more careful thought is needed to use it, which naturally brings about a more measured pace. Encouraging a cocktail-party client to sign key words while speaking may slow down the speech and at the same time point up the meaningful parts of the message. (A similar approach using symbols is described in Chapter 5.)

To introduce signing when a client can already speak may appear a retrograde step. In fact it parallels those occasions when one must apparently move backwards in order to make real progress. The bad habits of, say, typing must be painfully unlearned before a person's speed can be increased. Another analogy illustrates the importance of consciously practising a skill: police drivers are taught to improve their technique by giving a detailed spoken analysis of their thought processes as they drive along. Similarly, signing salient words while speaking encourages clients to analyse their communication and so better appreciate which parts of the content are relevant.

(For further reading, see 'The "Cocktail Party Syndrome" in Children with Hydrocephalus and Spina Bifida' (Tew 1979).)

Elective Mutism

An elective mute is a person who could speak, and possibly at some times or in some places has spoken or does speak, but for some reason chooses not to do so either some or all of the time. The withdrawal into non-speaking may be the result of emotional stress or disturbance, possibly brought about by a trauma or event which caused a sudden shock. Although the person's real ability may be normal or close to normal, his overt level of functioning may make him appear mentally handicapped.

Very occasionally the return of speech may be dramatic. More often, progress is slow, a little speech being coaxed out by someone who has formed a sympathetic relationship with the mute person and is trusted by him. A non-speech system can play a part in eliciting speech by fostering the habit of communication. As the client grows in confidence, he can be encouraged to speak the words that are signed or set down in symbol form, paving the way for more extended speech.

(For further reading, see 'Electively Mute Children: Psychological Development and Background Factors' (Kolvin and Fundudis 1981).)

Assessing the Client

The previous section looked at some of the conditions and characteristics of mentally handicapped people who might benefit from a non-speech system. This section discusses what further information will be necessary or useful when deciding on a particular system, on the appropriateness of methods and approaches, and on a suitable starting point for a teaching programme. In order to provide a baseline, it begins by briefly describing the normal sequence of language development.

Normal Language Development

From the time of his birth, a baby is able to cry in such a way that his mother can distinguish different messages conveyed by the cry, e.g. hunger or discomfort. By about four months, the baby is readily expressing more pleasurable feelings by cooing and chuckling, particularly in response to a familiar voice.

At six to nine months, he is babbling and producing a variety of sounds such as 'ma', 'ba' and 'da', often repeating them so that sounds/words like 'mama' and 'dada' can be distinguished. The intonation of normal speech becomes quite clearly marked and continuous babbling may sound like fragments of mature speech. The child enjoys getting a response from those around him, but also takes pleasure in simply making and controlling sound.

By twelve to eighteen months, the child has acquired a small number of more or less recognisable words which he uses meaningfully, though not necessarily correctly. (This is the age when, say, 'dog' might be applied equally well to a cat, or indeed to any other small animal with four legs.) He responds to 'no' and to a few simple commands in context, such as 'Wave goodbye' or 'Give me a kiss'.

Between the ages of eighteen months and two years there is a sudden spurt in the acquisition of vocabulary and the child probably knows about 200 words by the end of this period. He can point to more objects than he can name, can understand simple questions and is beginning to make up two-word phrases.

Over the next three months or so, the child's vocabulary increases to 300 to 400 words, including some prepositions and pronouns. He regularly uses two- and three-word phrases. About six months later, three- and four-word sentences are common, though grammar and sentence structure differ from those of adult speech.

By the time he is about three years old, simple sentences are grammatically well formed and the child's vocabulary has reached about a thousand words.

(For further reading, see *The Child's Acquisition of Language* (Derrick 1977), or, for a much more extended account, *A First Language: The Early Stages* (Brown 1973).)

The Prerequisites of Communication

A normally developing baby quickly learns to respond to and interact with another person, usually his mother, as it is she who usually has the most extended contact with him. This serves as a basis for later more complex communication. In parallel, assessment must be made of whether a prospective client can recognise intentional communication, for without this ability he has no foundation for acquiring a 'system', no matter how elementary. His ability may well be demonstrated non-verbally, for example by smiling in response to a smile, for this is sufficient evidence that he has understood the essential two-way nature of communication.

This example also illustrates the very earliest beginnings of 'symbolisation' or 'symbolic thought' in which one thing stands for another: the smiled-at person received the message of warm feeling conveyed by the smile and returned the same message. Symbolic thought may occur at a relatively concrete or highly abstract level. A baby who sees someone holding a cup and realises that a drink is on the way is engaging in symbolic thought. At a higher level comes the understanding that words (or signs or graphic symbols) are 'symbols' which represent something else, i.e. the 'real thing' or concept. All linguistic comprehension or expression is dependent on the ability to engage in symbolic thought.

To Speak or Not to Speak

A crucial issue is of course whether a non-speech system is necessary at all or whether it would be better to concentrate on speech alone. No hard-and-fast rules for resolving this can be given, for, quite apart from physical factors, much depends on individual personality and the inter-relationship between age (which is any case cannot be pinpointed), stage and situation. Professional assessment and advice need to be sought, but nevertheless certain features in a child's behaviour may be indicative of his future progress.

If a young handicapped child is beginning to make himself understood, perhaps using consistently a few 'words' that are meaningful at least to him, then he will probably not require non-speech assistance. Sometimes a child does not use words, but even so is babbling and taking an interest in sounds. Especially when this behaviour relates to his overall level of development, there is a good chance that speech will keep pace with other aspects. If, however, language development lags far behind the rest, then a non-speech system is more likely to be useful. This is undoubtedly so when professional medical opinion suggests that physical factors preclude the acquisition of speech or militate strongly against it. Similarly when an older client's attempts at speech are incomprehensible, and his physical condition seems to be responsible for the lack of clarity, an alternative system may facilitate effective communication.

We must stress again that introducing a non-speech system is not an all-or-nothing choice, a decision to be made once and for all. Many clients use a so-called alternative as no more than a support or augmentation of their speech – which despite being unclear or limited is still their primary means of communication. Besides, the linguistic framework of a non-speech system is more likely to stimulate than deter speech. Another theory advocating the learning of an alternative system points to the build-up of stress in individuals whose attempts at speech have failed over a longer period or who have been strongly pressured to talk. As attention is drawn away from their vocal efforts by their successful non-speech communication, the stress is released, the muscles relax and speech may at last be attainable. No teacher, speech therapist or other person introducing a non-speech system doubts that speech remains the ideal goal.

Personal Resources

Learning programmes, especially for a whole group of clients, would be easier to set up if each individual's likely speed of learning could be calculated. Unfortunately, no-one has yet found a foolproof method of doing this, and although there are many theories on factors relevant to success, they have not been isolated in a controlled experiment. While it is reasonable to expect a higher IQ to have an overall positive effect, the measurement of IQ is notoriously inexact and does not correlate precisely with attainment or ability to learn.

Motivation is a matter for observation rather than measurement, but very relevant since a well-motivated client has a head start over the rest. A client's way of life may indicate whether motivating him will be difficult or relatively easy. People's attitudes are conditioned by their environment and mentally handicapped (and other) people who are unaccustomed to doing anything for themselves are not motivated to make the attempt. If they lack experience in problem-solving, they are ill equipped to tackle new tasks, either of learning or of a practical nature.

A carer's good intentions in being as helpful as possible, perhaps with the associated aim of preventing distressing outbursts of frustration, have unhappy results in the longer term: firstly, the client comes to expect that his demands will automatically be met and never learns to control his frustration if they are not; secondly, he has no opportunity to acquire the skills of independence which can lead to a more fulfilled life; and thirdly, he actually learns to be helpless because his needs are attended to even when he remains completely passive (Seligman 1975). Some ways of increasing motivation will be suggested in Chapter 5, as will teaching approaches to suit the personality and behaviour of clients.

It must not be forgotten, moreover, that success may stimulate motivation. Many handicapped people only discover that they want to communicate once they have gained confidence when doing so effectively. Paula, a deaf mentally handicapped teenage girl known to one of the authors was taught how to sign the single word 'please'. Having formerly been withdrawn, unco-operative and seemingly unmotivated, she started to make frequent friendly contact with her teachers through small, easily granted requests, conveyed by the sign for 'please' plus an indication of the desired object. Not only did she obviously enjoy communicating, but her general willingness to learn also increased. Sad to say, she left school before her signing repertoire had extended very far (and in fact in her residential setting no signing was used). This is one instance when waiting until a client was 'ready' to learn would have meant a lost opportunity. Waiting over-long for 'readiness' is a trap to be avoided.

Observing a client's natural interests and aptitudes may influence the choice of system. Does he spontaneously use gestures as a form of communication or imitate the gestures of others? If so, he probably has an affinity for signing. Does he like looking at books or enjoy picture-matching activities? If so, then symbols may appeal. On the other hand, a client who has specific difficulties, in discriminating shapes or pictures will tend to find symbols a problem, and one who engages in continual stereotyped hand movements may be particularly unreceptive to signing until he has learnt some other form of occupation. (These and other points relevant to the selection of one or other type of system are summarised in Chapter 6.)

Physical Considerations

The physical handicaps of a number of potential clients who might benefit from a non-speech system have already been discussed. A general point has been made that the fine motor demands of signing, which often involve the use of both hands, may make symbols a natural choice for someone who is physically handicapped. For example, to start some symbol programmes, the only motor requirement is an ability to point with the eyes to indicate yes and no. Physical handicap does not, however, necessarily make signing impossible. The underlying aptitude of a person might in fact be for signing and his high level of motivation might lead to signs which were comprehensible even if only approximately correct. A school where one of the authors used to work successfully used the Paget Gorman Sign System with its cerebral-palsied pupils, who were also mentally handicapped.

Whatever programme is being undertaken, the overall well-being of a child with cerebral palsy and his optimum physical and motor development need careful consideration. Appropriate seating and positioning will be important. The specialist advice of physiotherapists and other occupational therapists can prove invaluable, and multi-disciplinary co-operation may be the secret of success in an apparently unpromising scheme. Future developments in computer software will open up further possibilities for physically handicapped clients, and in attempting to use a symbol system for communication they may be helped by a variety of accessing methods.

Communication and Language

Some differentiation must be made between communication and language, though the two are closely inter-connected.

Communication is the intentional conveying of a message, with or without language. This may be achieved non-verbally, i.e. without words or any other form of conventional language. It may also be done verbally; verbal communication involves words, which stand for particular concepts. Since signs and symbols also stand for particular concepts, they too can be used for verbal communication, though they are non-*vocal*, i.e. not spoken. Strictly speaking, in non-*vocal* communication linguistic concepts may or need not be involved, but some people use the term loosely, as synonymous with non-verbal. Therefore, to avoid possible confusion, we have used the term 'non-speech' to define non-spoken but linguistically based communication systems.

Obviously linguistic considerations become central whenever communication progresses beyond the non-verbal. Space does not permit a detailed discussion of tests and methods of assessing linguistic competence, but the simplified account which follows aims to give readers a general understanding of assessment strategies and underlying assumptions.

Assessment needs to distinguish between receptive language, which is sometimes referred to as comprehension and parallels 'inner language', and expressive language, which is language that a person produces himself. In normal development, expression usually lags behind comprehension, and everyone is familiar with small children who understand a great deal of what is said to them before they can talk themselves. When a person is mentally handicapped, the gap between comprehension and expression may be very wide. Spoken expression indeed may not occur at all, even when comprehension is quite adequate for day-to-day purposes. It is important that the distinction is taken into account, because otherwise teaching efforts may be dissipated on what is already understood.

An apparently quick success in establishing a small signed vocabulary, for example, may simply mean that a client has learned to sign on demand a number of words he already understands, not that he has acquired brand new vocabulary. Teachers may become frustrated unless they realise that meaningful gains will have to be based on more comprehensive language tuition, teaching the underlying concepts as well as the signs themselves. On the other hand, if teachers persuade a client to start signing spontaneously, remaining within the limits of his previously acquired receptive vocabulary, this is undoubtedly progress.

Even the simplest of receptive language – let alone any expressive capacity – may be beyond many non-speech candidates prior to teaching. However, useful information can often be attained using the following tests. The British Picture Vocabulary Test (Dunn, Leota, Whetton and Pintillie 1982) requires the subject to point to whichever picture out of four corresponds to each stimulus word spoken by the tester. The series of nouns, verbs and adjectives gradually increases in difficulty and testing continues until the subject reaches the ceiling of his comprehension. Scoring can be interpreted to give the subject's approximate age level (through a standardised score) and indicates the breadth of his receptive vocabulary. The Boehm Test of Basic Concepts (Boehm 1971), which is administered in a similar way except that the item tested is embedded in a short sentence, deals mainly with prepositions plus a few adverbs and adjectives. Incorrect answers to the Boehm Test are helpful in revealing specific conceptual gaps which can be attended to in teaching.

Assessment of a client's expression may stress either verbal language or broader communication skills. LARSP, i.e. Language Assessment, Remediation and Screening Procedures (Crystal, Fletcher and Garman 1976; see also Crystal 1979), compiles a subject's profile on the basis of a minute grammatical analysis of his verbal (spoken) language. This becomes more informative when speech has progressed beyond the very simplest utterances and LARSP can then be a very precise tool for use prior to 'remediation procedure'.

The intentions that a client is able to express within a particular communication can be assessed for practical purposes without a formal test. These illuminate a client's understanding of the nature and potential of communication. Can he demand something, for example, as well as drawing attention to it? Can he request recurrence ('more', 'again' or a non-verbal equivalent)? Can he ask a question (e.g. 'What's that?' or a non-verbal equivalent)? Can he express negatives, indicating rejection and/or non-existence (e.g. 'no want' = 'I don't want it', 'no boy' = 'The boy's not here', or equivalent non-verbal expression such as empty spread hands or appropriate facial expression)? It should not be forgotten how important body language and expression are in conveying intention. A wide range of intentions is an excellent basis for developing the use of a communication system, either non-speech or speech, but if assessment finds the range to be limited at least it has identified what is known and unknown, so that teaching and language practice can be directed accordingly.

The Reynell Developmental Language Scales (Reynell 1977) are composed of one scale for comprehension and one for expression. These can be used independently of each other. Scoring assigns an age to the subject equivalent to normal language competence. More specific than the Reynell Scales is the Carrow Test for Auditory Comprehension (Carrow 1973) which samples the subject's ability to understand certain grammatical constructions. The Sentence Comprehension Test (Wheldall, Mittler and Hobsbaum 1979) also measures comprehension of specific constructions in sentences of increasing length and complexity. These three tests are 'closed', i.e. they may only be administered by psychologists and others with special qualifications.

Some of the ideas in these closed tests can be adopted and adapted for outside use. Even if a standardised score cannot be found by this method, it is possible to diagnose areas of non-comprehension or of competence already achieved. The chosen non-speech system can then be taught at a level to suit a client's inner or receptive language.

The essential technique of the tests is to give a cue representing the grammatical structure that is being assessed. Response to the cue involves selecting from a number of pictorial or three-dimensional alternatives, one of which corresponds to the cue while the others deviate in different ways. (Before a non-speech system has been introduced, the cue will be spoken; later assessments might make use of non-speech cues. Of course, this would not test *auditory* comprehension.)

The aim might be, for example, to assess how well a client understood the sentence 'The cat is under the table.' His correct response would be to select the corresponding picture B (see Figure 1.1). Any other response would need interpretation in order to reveal the particular type of confusion or deficit which might require attention in a teaching programme.

Figure 1.1: Array of Pictures for Selection to Assess Comprehension of a Verbal Cue

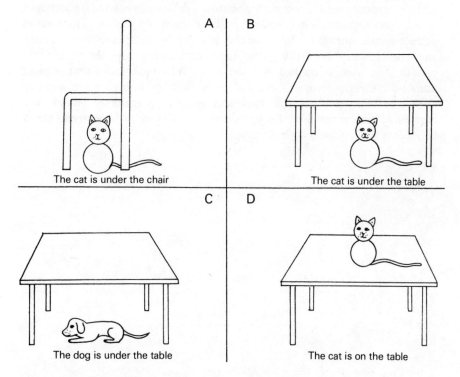

If he chooses picture A, he may have understood the cue only as far as the word 'cat' (or only attended up to that point), and simply selected the first picture showing a cat. Alternatively, within this sentence structure he may only have been able to cope with two information-bearing words, 'cat' and 'under', and forgotten or failed to process the third word 'table'. Choice of picture C may be similarly explained by an overload of information; in another less complex sentence the client might have distinguished perfectly well between the words 'dog' and 'cat' – though the mistake in this instance could also be accounted for by very basic vocabulary confusion. Choosing picture D would suggest that the client has understood the nouns, but ignored or misunderstood the preposition 'under'. Further testing would establish whether this was a general difficulty with prepositions or whether it was specific to this word.

Of course there is always the possibility that the client is responding at random. We can, however, check for this by including several similar items in one test and noting whether the responses are consistent.

Tests are by definition narrower than the collection of data by general observation, and a client's needs are wider than simply vocabulary or grammatical construction. Communication in the broadest sense can be verbal or non-verbal, covering intention, facial expression, body language, specific gesture, response to others in various settings, different types and frequency of initiated contact, etc. – the whole gamut of social interaction. This overall pattern is affected by aptitude, ability, personality, the home or residential environment, the school or work or leisure environment, and the people who care for and come in contact with the client. Information about all of these allows a clearer picture of the client to be built up during assessment and should be taken into account when setting up a programme. To set up a communication programme for one person in isolation, whose needs are ill defined, is hardly likely to bear fruit.

2 MANUAL SIGNING AND SIGNING SYSTEMS

In this chapter we begin by looking at the development of manual signing as a means of communication and some of the reasons why a mentally handicapped person may learn signing more easily than speech. The major part of the chapter is devoted to a description and discussion of individual systems, followed by a brief comparison of their different characteristics.

The Use of Body Language

Many hypotheses on the development of speech by the human race attribute a key role to the use of the body. The most basic emotional and social body language is instinctive, its manifestations resembling the body language of animals, for example the postures of aggression or fear and the close physical approaches that signify friendliness. Some suggest that in primitive times ideas came to be linked with arbitrary vocalised symbols (i.e. elementary words) through gestures, which facilitated a readier understanding of rudimentary but developing spoken language.

Gesture, which is a more ritualised form of body language, varies culturally to a wider extent than basic body language. Some gestures are confined to specific situations and may evolve in meaning, coming to signify different things to people from different cultures or geographical locations. (One of the authors discovered, for example, that a familiar gesture which offers an offensive insult in Britain, was quite unknown – and therefore inoffensive – to friends in Germany.) People of all cultures make use of gesture to expand or emphasise the verbal message.

Gestures can also express more defined concepts, such as direction by means of pointing, actions through demonstration, and past and future time by indicating backwards and forwards. It is possible too to give absent objects some kind of pseudo-visual form by drawing an outline sketch of them in the air.

Codified Gesture and Sign Systems

In modern times, in situations where speech cannot serve the purpose, specific signals for conveying basic information have developed from gesture. At British race meetings, for example, the tick tack man uses manual signals to pass messages about betting odds across distances over which speech would not be heard. In North America in the nineteenth century Indian tribes with different languages, who came into regular but occasional contact, evolved a code of 'hand talk' in order to exchange information. From this hand talk the therapeutic system of Amer-Ind has been devised to help stroke victims and others with impaired speech.

Signalled codes convey a quite narrow range of messages, unlike the languages of manual signs which have developed within deaf communities of the world. These are capable of conveying precise and complex information and, just as every spoken language has its conventional grammar and word order, so does every sign language. Sign order may be unrelated to the word order of speech.

Some signs in sign languages have iconic features, i.e. they are to some extent representational, visually suggesting or resembling the meaning of the sign. This parallels onomatopoeic spoken words like 'splash' or 'cuckoo', which *sound* like the meaning of the word. As a general principle, however, signs (like words) are arbitrary and no more universally understandable than are spoken words to speakers of a different language. They do not even have the shared roots that occur in, say, the various Romance languages in Europe.

Sign languages of many nations continue to evolve in the course of use by deaf people. Among them are American Sign Language (ASL), which is derived from Old French Sign Language, was imported to the USA by a Frenchman and still contains some elements of French signing grammar. In the UK British Sign Language (BSL) was evolved by the deaf community.

Some educationalists have felt that a signing system was needed which precisely mirrored spoken language and have devised systems for this purpose. One such is the Paget Gorman Sign System (PGSS), named after its inventor and developers. Another is Signed English (SE). Developed initially in the USA and subsequently in the UK, SE incorporates the signs of ASL and BSL respectively.

Another system using signs from BSL is the Makaton Vocabulary, devised in the UK specifically for use with mentally handicapped people. Makaton is signed using key words only, in the word order of speech, rather in the manner of a pidgin language.

Sign language, sign systems and speech can be seen as belonging to a continuum, depending on their closeness to 'total' signing or 'total' speech. They also divide according to whether they are a language with their own grammatical identity or whether they are a system of speech coding. (See Figure 2.1, noting that Amer-Ind, as a sign code, does not appear.)

Figure 2.1: A Continuum of Language Systems

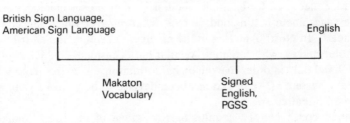

Natural languages

British Sign Language,
American Sign Language   English

Makaton   Signed
Vocabulary   English,
                 PGSS

Systems of coding English

Each of the sign systems mentioned above that is in use in the UK (for convenience, the sign languages, systems and sign code will be referred to collectively as 'systems') will be described in later sections of this chapter; all have come to be used with mentally handicapped people. A short section on finger spelling has also been included in order to clarify the way it differs from sign systems. No section on ASL in included as its use is confined to the USA. Readers wishing for further information on this system might refer to 'The Linguistics of Manual Language and Manual Systems' (Wilbur 1976).

Learning to Sign

Mentally handicapped people who have failed to acquire useful speech may learn to communicate effectively by signing. In the development of the human race, gesture was an early and natural expression; so it is in a child and mentally handicapped people may never reach beyond a child's immature level of development. Pointing at a desired object is common in children from the age of about eight months, well before mature speech emerges. Piaget (1970) theorises concerning the developmental pattern of a child that action is an essential basis for later speech. He suggests that a child in his thinking comes to internalise the actions that he has performed many times. Gesture, which partially represents action, is therefore a stepping stone to the symbolic thought that is necessary for meaningful speech. (Symbolic thought is discussed more fully at the beginning of Chapter 3.)

When a mentally handicapped person already uses natural gesture, teaching can concentrate on systematising this into signing. Even when gesture has not developed, the process of teaching a person to sign is still less complex than teaching him to speak. The teacher (or therapist or parent or carer) can 'mould' the client's hands to form signs. Gradually the amount of intervention can be faded as the client learns to form each sign independently.

Moulding is not feasible for the hidden and inaccessible organs of speech production and, though moulding of the lips is less impracticable, in fact they retain virtually the same shape for distinctly different sounds (e.g. t, d, g, k, h). With signs, which are more visually distinctive, clients can be given the opportunity to observe and imitate another person's handshapes – a transitional stage between the passive acceptance of moulding and independent sign production.

Clients may be helped to remember the different sign postures through the gross motor involvement of hands and arms in signing, as well as through the sense of touch when hands come in contact with each other or with other parts of the body. The movement may also facilitate comprehension since the senses and thinking processes are more stimulated by watching activity than by looking at something which does not move.

The fact that some signs are iconic is another possible aid to comprehension. Their visual resemblance to what they signify may serve as a reminder both of the meaning and their formation.

(For further reading, see 'Signs of Speech: Cooperating in Deaf Education' (Kyle 1982).)

Having considered a number of reasons why mentally handicapped people may learn to sign more easily than to speak, we shall now look at individual sign systems and their characteristics. Following the description of each system, certain specifically relevant issues will be raised, under the heading of 'discussion points'.

Amer-Ind

Amer-Ind (or Amerind), although included within the category of signing systems, is better described as a gestural code of signals. The set of 236 signals and its clinical usage have been developed in the USA by Madge Skelly, a speech pathologist, for patients with a range of communication handicaps. Most of Skelly's initial work was with adults who had lost the ability to speak after a stroke or other brain trauma, but the system has also been used to help mentally handicapped people with language difficulties.

Skelly, herself an Indian, developed Amer-Ind from the hand talk of American Indians, whose different tribes, each with its own distinct language, needed a simple, clear, unambiguous form of communication with which to conduct periodic trade negotiations. The hand talk which evolved for this purpose was capable of transmitting the necessary broad concepts. From the memories of older Indians, plus some written information on hand talk, Amer-Ind was formulated as a code for basic non-speech communication in a therapeutic setting.

Handshapes of the majority of signals are simple and naturally assumed, for example a flat hand or a pointed index finger. Over half of them are performed with only one hand. They are divided into categories according to the method of execution. For a *static* signal the hand position is held (see Figure 2.2). A *kinetic* signal involves movement (see Figure 2.3). A *repetitive* signal repeats a particular movement (see Figure 2.4).

The signal categories are not related to meaning; for example, the verb ADD is a static signal, while the signal for TABLE is kinetic. In any case signals cut across parts of speech, as in Figure 2.4, where the signal for BABY or YOUNGSTER can equally well mean (TO) SPOIL or (TO) PAMPER (i.e. (TO) BABY). Obviously, therefore, there is no set signal-for-word transposition between Amer-Ind and spoken English. Transposition is also impracticable on account of 'agglutination', which is the process by which basic signals can be 'stuck together' in order to signify something new. For example, WALK + IN = ENTER and (as in Figure 2.5) WALK + LOOK + PERSON = GUIDE.

The PERSON signal is one of the very few Amer-Ind markers. (A marker is

Figure 2.2: Amer-Ind Static Signals

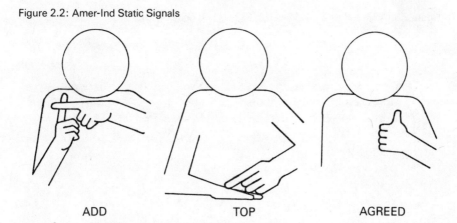

ADD   TOP   AGREED

Figure 2.3: Amer-Ind Kinetic Signals

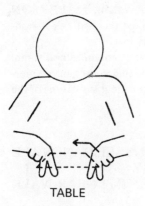

TABLE   HERE   ABOVE

Figure 2.4: Amer-Ind Repetitive Signals

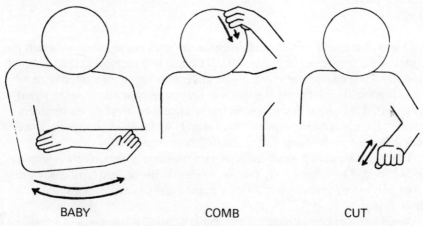

BABY   COMB   CUT

(The action for each signal is repeated three times.)

Figure 2.5: Amer-Ind — Agglutination of Signals to Signify GUIDE

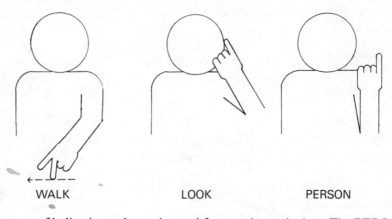

WALK　　　　　　　　LOOK　　　　　　　PERSON

a means of indicating a change in word-form, or its equivalent. The PERSON marker indicated -ER in such a word as SINGER or the equivalent non-verbally signified person in the noun-signal GUIDE.)

Amer-Ind has no predetermined rules for structuring sentences and signal order is left to teachers or users to decide. Skelly urges that coding into Amer-Ind should employ a simple telegraphic style following a clear logic. One of the examples she gives is as follows:

Spoken English	*Amer-Ind*
Almost all people who see	ALL PERSONS SEE HAND TALK
Amer-Ind understand it	KNOW EASY
easily. Let us limit	CHOP TALK TIME NEAR WALK
comments to brief	EAT.
statements so we may	
adjourn promptly for	
lunch.	

One of Amer-Ind's most notable characteristics is the extent to which its signals are transparent (i.e. guessable). Research suggests that at least half and possibly three-quarters or more can be understood by an untrained observer, on account of their iconicity (i.e. the way they suggest or resemble the signal's meaning). This means that people in the handicapped person's environment – parents, friends or professionals – may readily understand his signals, even if they have not participated in the training programme.

The transparency of Amer-Ind may also facilitate communication with the wider world. This is especially relevant in view of the present trend away from large institutions towards smaller, more community-based establishments for daily living.

Amer-Ind was first introduced into the UK in 1978 by means of a training workshop. Since then further training workshops have been held in England and Scotland; these normally last for five days and cover the whole system. In 1979 Skelly published a comprehensive volume describing the system, also giving teaching strategies, other related information and summaries of research projects. Her Scale of Progress from this volume has been adapted by Daniloff and Shafer (1981) to form their 'gestural communication programme for severely-profoundly handicapped children', which gives an easy-to-follow outline of the steps they used to teach gestures to this population.

Discussion Point 1:

> *'Mentally handicapped users of Amer-Ind will be hampered by the non-specific nature of its signals and its lack of grammatical structure.'*

Proponents of Amer-Ind suggest that one of the system's strengths is the breadth of its signal-concepts. These have integrity of meaning without narrow linguistic definition and can convey a message with great economy of expression. As concepts can be communicated through several different meaning-routes, they can be made more specific, for example by adding extra information to the initial signal by agglutination or by the 'negative affirmative contrast' (Skelly 1979) which emphasises what a concept is by showing what it is not.

The structure of a communication is subordinate to its meaning in Amer-Ind, so the user is free to concentrate on his message without having to concern himself with grammatical correctness. This procedure may be quite sophisticated enough and appropriate for mentally handicapped users, whose expression often resembles the pre-grammatical expression of children.

Discussion Point 2:

> *'The limited size of the Amer-Ind vocabulary means that it is suitable for mentally handicapped users.'*

Although the number of basic signals is limited to 236, the size of the vocabulary is effectively larger because each signal can stand for several related concepts. However, Lloyd and Daniloff (1983) point out that no distinction is possible between, for example, APPLE, CANDY, COOKIE, EAT and SPOON, which could cause difficulties for some handicapped people operating at a very concrete level. Despite its small size, not all the vocabulary is functional for a mentally handicapped person, who might easily manage without, say, JUSTICE or POMPOUS, which are included, but would very likely want APPLE and TOILET, which are not. Because the concepts are broad, there are no signals to relate to an individual's special interests, and creating new signals by agglutination may be too demanding a strategy for some users.

It is the relevance of a vocabulary and not its size that makes it suitable for particular users, and of course Amer-Ind was devised for non-speaking but cognitively normal clients. Naturally, if other aspects of the system made it an appropriate choice for a mentally handicapped client then the required signs could be borrowed from another system, even though this might disturb the conceptual principles of the Amer-Ind code.

Discussion Point 3:

> *'Amer-Ind is especially appropriate for clients with only limited use of their hands.'*

We have already mentioned that the handshapes of Amer-Ind signals are in general simple and naturally assumed, requiring few fine finger movements. The number of exceptions to this is very limited. About half the total number of signals are located in the most convenient place for signing with the hands, i.e. just in front of the body, and only a very few are located in a significantly inconvenient place.

Perhaps even more relevant is the fact that over half the signals can be performed using one hand only, without the other being involved at all. In addition, virtually all the rest have been adapted by Skelly (1979) so that they too can be performed one-handedly. It is of course possible to adapt other systems similarly, but the Amer-Ind adaptation is clearly documented and readily available to teachers and therapists. The system does therefore lend itself to being used by clients with only limited hand use.

Discussion Point 4:

> *'The lack of prescribed structure means that Amer-Ind is unlikely to promote or support speech.'*

The signals of Amer-Ind do not stand for particular words and the vocabulary does not incorporate grammatical function words (e.g. in the following, the italicised function words and morphemes are omitted: '*Will* we *be going to* stay?') However, because a user can choose the signal order, it is quite possible to arrange the signal-concepts in the same order as speech-concepts and to use the two together (or, as Skelly recommends, immediately precede the words with the signals).

Daniloff and Shafer (1981) note that many of the mentally handicapped children they trained to use signals who began to sign spontaneously also vocalised quite extensively. Children who learned to combine signals were beginning to use recognisable words too. No specific speech training had been given, so it is a reasonable conclusion that the use of Amer-Ind stimulated the use of speech. Although no data is provided on whether or how the speech was structured, there is certainly no indication that Amer-Ind's lack of formal grammar inhibited speech production.

British Sign Language and Signed Coding of English

British Sign Language or BSL, the natural language of the deaf community in the UK, has evolved over centuries in the course of use. As discussed earlier in the chapter, it shares a number of characteristics with spoken languages. Unlike these, however, it is often not the first language learned at home, as many deaf children are born to parents with normal hearing. In the past, many of these children have had difficulty in getting to know BSL at school owing to the widely held view that its use might discourage speech and was therefore undesirable. Deaf children, anxious to communicate with their peers more effectively than they found possible with speech, were forced to pick up BSL clandestinely and to use it in secret.

Attitudes are softening as educators come to appreciate the ways in which using a sign language can facilitate communication. Firstly, it gives deaf children a firm linguistic base on which to build their learning of a second language, i.e. spoken English, and secondly, it is an integral part of Total Communication. In accordance with these principles, one British school educates its profoundly deaf, moderately mentally handicapped pupils bilingually; they are taught BSL and spoken English as two quite separate languages.

Though individual signs can be generally defined with a word meaning, there is no precise sign-word match between the two languages. Because signing is located in space, concepts are expressed differently and sometimes more economically than in the spoken language. For example, the voice can only represent things in sequence, whereas a sign can simultaneously represent an object and a particular characteristic of it, so that, say, BIG BALL simply requires BALL to be signed in a large manner.

Signs in BSL

The majority of handshapes of BSL signs are quite 'natural' (e.g. flat hand and fist) and easy to assume. Some research (reported in Kiernan, Jordan and Saunders 1978) suggests that about half of the signs in everyday use are performed by only one hand; over a third use two hands in the same symmetrical position.

Although in principle the signs are arbitrary, there are iconic features in some signs which take a variety of forms. Figure 2.6 illustrates three signs in which a picture is presented by the hands. Some signs, as illustrated in Figure 2.7, are direct mimes of an activity. Often these signs are represented variably in terms of a context rather than in a standardised form; for example, the stirring motion of COOK in Figure 2.7 might be performed as if over a pan instead of a bowl as illustrated.

Some signs were originally pictographic, but the meaningful link is now forgotten. For example, SUGAR in Figure 2.8 formerly suggested the facial dermatitis that deaf Liverpool dockers contracted as a result of unloading sacks of sugar. BISCUIT in the same figure is said to represent

Figure 2.6: British Sign Language Iconic Signs

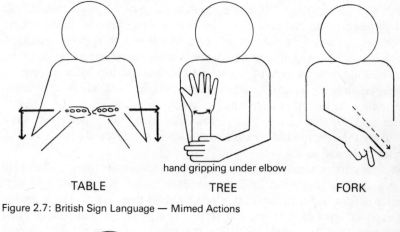

hand gripping under elbow

TABLE   TREE   FORK

Figure 2.7: British Sign Language — Mimed Actions

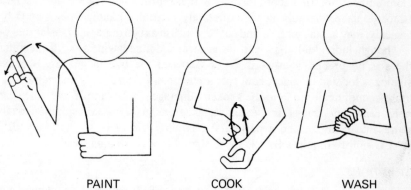

PAINT   COOK   WASH

Figure 2.8: British Sign Language Signs Involving Now Obsolete Iconic Elements

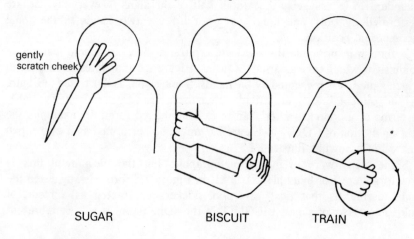

gently
scratch cheek

SUGAR   BISCUIT   TRAIN

Figure 2.9: British Sign Language Abstract Signs

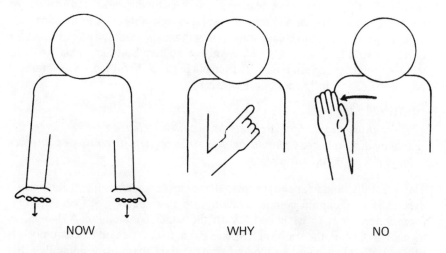

NOW   WHY   NO

sailors knocking weevils out of old-fashioned ship's biscuits, and TRAIN mimics the pistons of a steam train, which bears no resemblance to a modern high-speed diesel.

Other signs signifying more abstract ideas are naturally more arbitrary; see, for example, WHY in Figure 2.9. Nevertheless, even some undeniably abstract signs can be seen to have roots in natural gesture, cf. NOW and NO in the same figure.

A few semantic (i.e. to do with meaning) conventions operate in BSL. Signs that are made near the forehead, for example, are frequently concerned with thinking, and many signs performed near the chest or stomach are to do with feeling.

In BSL, very often the tense of a verb or the number of a noun is not signed at all, the meaning being implicit in the context. However, to give one example of BSL grammar, the plural BISCUITS can either be expressed by finger-spelling 's' after the basic sign (see also the section on finger spelling later in this chapter) or alternatively by signing BISCUIT twice in quick succession.

(For further reading, see *Sign and Say* (RNID 1981), *Perspectives on British Sign Language and Deafness* (Kyle, Woll and Deuchar 1981) and 'Learning and Using BSL' (Kyle, Woll and Llewellyn-Jones 1981).)

Discussion Point 1:

   'BSL as a natural language of deaf people is the most suitable non-speech system for mentally handicapped people in the UK who are also deaf.'

Since aural (i.e. heard) forms of language are not accessible to deaf people, the deaf community replaces them with equally coherent visual forms. The fact that non-deaf mentally handicapped people quite often respond to a visual system is a strong indication that those with additional deafness are likely to benefit. BSL then appears a very suitable choice of system. However, if other members of the group are not deaf, then priorities for choice should be weighed up, since the sharing of a common system is desirable in practical terms.

An important point to bear in mind is that language teaching programmes for clients should suit their level of cognitive ability. Suitable goals for BSL teaching might therefore require the language to be simplified. (See comment on simplification in Discussion Point 2.)

Discussion Point 2:

'If mentally handicapped clients have failed to learn one language, i.e. spoken English, they should be given the opportunity to learn another language of equal status.'

For mentally handicapped people, the purpose of learning a non-speech system is to facilitate communication with their peers, with carers and – increasingly, it is to be hoped – with the wider community. Although, as already indicated, the status of BSL has risen, to the speaking community it is still an unfamiliar language. Not only are the signs themselves unfamiliar, but when decoded they are in a 'foreign' word order. If clients do begin to grasp mature BSL, there is the possibility that any spoken words might mirror the signs in non-English word order. This would result in idiosyncratic speech, which would reduce comprehensibility and 'normality'.

Failure of mentally handicapped people to learn speech may not only be due to the mechanics of speaking, but at least partly to its linguistic complexities. While BSL does not share these in *form*, in *nature* its own are not radically different. Simplification of BSL is possible, and telegraphic signing can be used and understood in the same way as children's telegraphic speech. But this form of signing, while functional, is no longer 'proper' BSL: rather it is a form of sign code utilising BSL signs.

(Note that arguments applicable to BSL in the UK might equally well apply to ASL in the USA.)

Many teachers consider it preferable that mentally handicapped people, especially those without hearing problems, should learn a speech-related signing system. We will therefore turn to two speech-related derivatives of BSL, that is Signed English and the Makaton Vocabulary.

Signed English

Signed English, or SE, is a way of visually representing the patterns of spoken English, including both content words and grammatical function words and morphemes. (A morpheme is the smallest distinctive grammatical unit that carries meaning, including inflections such as -ing and 's.) A set of 14 sign markers indicate changes in word-form; in other words, they stand for the grammatical morphemes. SE signing can be directly transposed into spoken English and used simultaneously with it.

SE was first developed in the USA during the 1970s by Harry Bornstein and others at Gallaudet College. It was based on signs drawn from ASL with additional sign markers. Many signs were modified to incorporate initial letters finger-spelled according to the American manual alphabet. *The Comprehensive Signed English Dictionary* (Bornstein, Saulnier and Hamilton) was published in 1983, illustrated with more than 3000 signs.

In the UK a working party on SE was set up in 1980, consisting mainly of staff from schools for the deaf and a number of deaf adults. By that time, several British schools and other establishments for the deaf had adopted BSL-based SE and one of the working party's aims was to standardise usage. In 1984 it published the first volume of *Signed English for Schools* (Working Party on Signed English 1984), incorporating a vocabulary of function words which provide the structure of the language. Volume 2 will follow, bringing the number of signs up to about 1500. The Working Party states that these comprise a basic vocabulary for daily use by young normal children. It makes the point that, within an educational setting, SE can help children become more competent in their use of spoken and conventionally written English through exposing them to a parallel visual form of it; BSL on the other hand is likely to be used by deaf children and adults outside the classroom as it is a more natural and economical system for communication.

Discussion Point 1:

'SE, with all its inflectional markers, is too complex for use by mentally handicapped people.'

SE can be modified for severely language-impaired users, including mentally handicapped people, by initially omitting inflectional markers altogether. When a client becomes more skilled in the use of SE, he can begin to introduce them, extending their use as far as he can linguistically cope with them. In the other direction, SE can be simplified and reduced in range as far as is necessary to suit the client. Even in a telegraphic or pidgin form of English it is still possible to present a meaningful spoken-and-signed message to a client in anticipation of a signed-only response of equal simplicity.

Discussion Point 2:

'As British SE is not yet widely established, at the moment it has little relevance as a non-speech system for mentally handicapped people.'

The use of SE, incorporated within the philosophy of Total Communication, is rapidly becoming more widespread at deaf schools in the UK. The spread is likely to be accelerated by the publication in 1984 of the first volume of *Signed English for Schools* (Working Party on Signed English 1984), as referred to earlier. At the same time, courses on SE are becoming more common, so the system is more readily accessible to those who wish to implement its use, not only with deaf clients, but also with mentally handicapped clients. In the USA it is increasingly often recommended for use by mentally handicapped people and some attractive ASL-based teaching materials have been developed there. Similar BSL-based materials would be equally appropriate in a UK context.

SE can be used at quite sophisticated or at very simple levels and so may be suitable for clients with a range of ability. Such flexibility is a feature which may appeal to those considering its use with mentally handicapped people. As a criterion for choice, this is certainly more relevant than whether or not it is widely established at the present time.

Discussion Point 3:

> *'SE offers to mentally handicapped users the dual advantage of supporting grammatical spoken English and of facilitating communication with the deaf community.'*

SE can precisely reflect the patterns of mature spoken English, but since few mentally handicapped people will ever attain comprehensive use of the markers, their signing will represent only a telegraphic or pidgin form of spoken English. On the other hand, SE does have the potential to support grammatical speech if the user should progress that far.

Regarding its use in the UK, incorporated in British SE are a number of changes in meaning of BSL signs (known as 'generated signs'). These, along with grammatical markers and signs sequenced in the order of speech, will make SE look somewhat strange to the eyes of a BSL signer and in a few cases misunderstandings might occur.

However, these possible difficulties are as nothing compared to the advantages: firstly, there is theoretically no ceiling to the development of the mentally handicapped users' sign-supported spoken English; secondly, they have the opportunity to learn a sign system broadly comprehensible to a quite different section of the population (i.e. the deaf) which has not required any special training in the context of mentally handicapped people. The authors have seen simple but greatly enjoyed signed communication between a little boy in a nursery class for severely mentally handicapped children and a visiting teenager from a partially hearing unit.

The Makaton Vocabulary

The Makaton Vocabulary is a set of some 350 words represented by BSL signs. The term 'Makaton' is derived from the names of the three people who originally devised the vocabulary and associated research project for a group of deaf mentally handicapped adults living in hospital. MArgaret Walker was the Senior Speech Therapist at the hospital, and KAthy Johnston and TONy Cornforth were Psychiatric Hospital Visitors from the Royal Association for the Deaf and Dumb.

The vocabulary is divided into eight stages, said to be arranged in developmental order, plus a ninth stage for specific additional items needed by individuals. The stages make up a language programme, according to which clients should learn Stage 1 before progressing to Stage 2, and so on. The initial vocabulary was based on the word usage of a group of severely mentally handicapped institutionalised adults (Mein and O'Connor 1960); the Revised Makaton Vocabulary (Walker 1976) includes extra items relevant to children's school and home environment. The size of the whole is restricted so that it forms a basis for communication and language learning, containing words/signs that easily combine into short phrases.

Alongside Makaton, the able person uses full grammatical speech and all relevant techniques of Total Communication. The signs accompany key words, appearing in the same order as they are spoken; it is thus mainly the meaning-based content words that are signed as distinct from the grammatical function words that define the language structure.

Walker (1973) describes the positive findings of the research project in terms of number of signs learnt and improvements in vocalisation, eye-contact, attention and general sociability. She also notes that previously difficult behaviour was reduced. Although some doubt has been cast on the scientific rigour of the research (e.g. Bailey 1978), the Makaton Vocabulary remains an important milestone in the development of signing for mentally handicapped people.

Since the time of the original research, Walker has set up the Makaton Vocabulary Development Project, of which she is the director. One aspect of the project's work is the production of materials, including such items as a teaching manual, illustrations of signs in a dictionary and on individual cards, and photographs depicting objects listed in the vocabulary. Another aspect is an extensive organisation of workers in the field whose role is to arrange workshops to instruct teachers, speech therapists and others in Makaton and to provide ongoing advice and support to those using it. (For examination of the training methods recommended for teaching non-speakers to use Makaton, see Byler 1985).

Recently, there has been an attempt to link up the Makaton Vocabulary with Blissymbols (see Chapter 3, under that heading). A set of Rebus symbols (see Chapter 3) corresponding to the Makaton Vocabulary have also been designed: these are known as 'Makaton symbols'. Some ideas for teaching signs and symbols in combination will be described in Chapter 5.

Discussion Point 1:

'Learning to use the Makaton Vocabulary will help clients to develop either BSL or spoken English.'

BSL is a language possessing its own sign order and grammatical structure, whereas Makaton signs, though drawn from BSL, follow the word order of spoken English. However, only key words are signed and the grammatical morphemes are omitted. Thus, although related to both BSL and English, Makaton represents a pidgin form of both. It does not, therefore, directly support the mature form of either language.

A client who has acquired Makaton has a signing system at his disposal, which is functional in conveying simple messages. Makaton is, however, very limited compared with BSL in both flexibility and extent, because of its prescribed vocabulary and lack of structure, though its range may be adequate for a large number of mentally handicapped people.

The teacher or therapist, speaking full grammatical English while she signs, provides a speech model for the client. Nevertheless, if he learns to speak, his active practice of telegraphic-type Makaton may be mirrored by a telegraphic form of English.

Discussion Point 2:

'*The need to adhere to Stages 1 to 8 of the vocabulary is* vital.'

Such adherence used to be strongly prescribed in the Makaton philosophy (Walker 1978), but a more flexible approach is now accepted. However, the stated purpose of adhering to the stages was to follow normal language development, which presupposed the strict developmental ordering of the stages. At least one researcher (Kiernan 1977) has queried whether this is actually so. Even a layman might wonder, for example, why BISCUIT (Stage 1) appears two whole developmental stages before APPLE (Stage 3); BOAT (3) appears before WATER (4), although MILK and TEA appear in Stage 2. A word for expressing a very important early intention, WANT, does not appear until Stage 5, two stages after HAVE (3). Other examples of equally doubtful developmental order could be quoted.

As stated in the section on assessment in Chapter 1, the concepts and syntactic structures being taught to the client should suit his level of development or he may become confused. Walker's precept quite rightly aims to prevent this and adhering to the stages may help. On the other hand, departure from the stages into the uncharted realms of words/signs outside the Makaton Vocabulary will not prove disastrous if the alternative vocabulary is chosen with due attention to the client's needs and ability. It might even be more stimulating, relevant and effective.

Though the restrictions of the vocabulary seem somewhat artificial and inflexible, they may be helpful in two ways: (1) the stages offer a viable framework for both workshops and teaching programmes for clients (irrespective of their intrinsic validity); (2) professionals and others sometimes overwhelm a mentally handicapped person by too extensive a use of language. Observing the limits of the vocabulary cuts down the range and number of words used and may assist comprehension by highlighting meaningful content words.

Discussion Point 3:

> *'As the Makaton Vocabulary is so popular in the UK for use with mentally handicapped people, in the interest of standardisation it should be adopted in preference to any other signing system.'*

Theoretically, and at a bureaucratic level, standardisation may seem desirable. This way there may be less pressure on administrators who do not have to cope with a series of different approaches or a challenge to accepted ideas. A single project can be more efficiently supported. Some people may find it reassuring to know that they are part of a wider scheme.

However, standardisation inevitably excludes innovation, which often takes place when a particular initiative meets the needs of the moment – as did Makaton's signing initiative for mentally handicapped people at the beginning of the 1970s. Now and in the future, new needs requiring new approaches may arise.

Mentally handicapped people are not standardised and their individual patterns of need differ. So although many have been helped to communicate by using Makaton, it is not necessarily the best system for all (particularly the relatively high flyers). No research so far conducted would support such a claim by any system.

The problems of non-standardisation are often exaggerated. In this context, the most frequently mentioned is that of an individual transferring from one establishment to another, where he may find a different system in use. In fact, clients who have already acquired a communicative framework of signing will probably be able to adapt to an alternative vocabulary without great difficulty. Clients without such a firm framework, who have made little progress in their use of a system, may hardly be aware if a change takes place anyway.

If the appropriateness of a system for a particular client or group of clients is duly considered, then freedom of choice is preferable to standardisation. What is more, the benefits that may accrue from accepting a new idea can never be calculated in advance.

The Paget Gorman Sign System

The Paget Gorman Sign System, or PGSS, aims to provide an accurate signed representation of the English language, including its grammatical features. In 1934, in response to a request from the Senior Chaplain of the Royal Association of the Deaf and Dumb that he should devise a sign system to assist the language development of deaf people, Sir Richard Paget started work. His 'New Sign System' was devised in accordance with the belief, acquired during his research into existing sign language, that in the evolution of communication pantomimic signing was the natural precursor of mouth gestures, i.e. speech.

After Sir Richard's death, his wife and a Frenchman by the name of Pierre Gorman, himself deaf, revised and modified the original work. In recognition of Gorman's role in this, in 1971 their 'Systematic Sign Language' was renamed the Paget Gorman Sign System, and very recently Paget Gorman Signed Speech. The current version is published in a manual which gives precise and detailed instructions for performing over 3000 signs (Paget, Gorman and Paget 1976).

Figure 2.10: Paget Gorman Sign System Standard Hand Postures

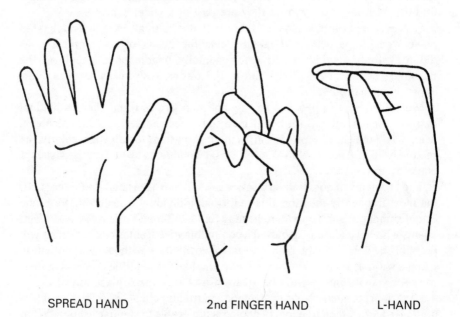

SPREAD HAND   2nd FINGER HAND   L-HAND

The formation of PGSS signs is based on 21 standard hand postures which appear regularly. Examples of these can be seen in Figure 2.10, from which it is evident that some of the hand postures are not natural or even particularly easy to assume. Relevant to meaning, there are in addition 37 basic signs representing basic concepts, such as COLOUR, ANIMAL or BUILDING. These signs employ one hand in specific postures and orientations. The meaning can be modified to a specific related concept by way of an extra component to the sign being added by the second hand. An example of the process can be seen in Figure 2.11.

In the PGSS manual, the abbreviated formula for the sign RED appears as follows: 'Hold 1st h as COLOUR and at same time with 2nd h S. BLOOD.' This can be expanded to 'Hold the first hand in the basic sign position that signifies COLOUR, and at the same time, with the second hand, make the sign BLOOD – instructions for which will be found in the manual under that word.'

Figure 2.11: Paget Gorman Sign System Hand Posture + Signifier to Make Up the Sign RED

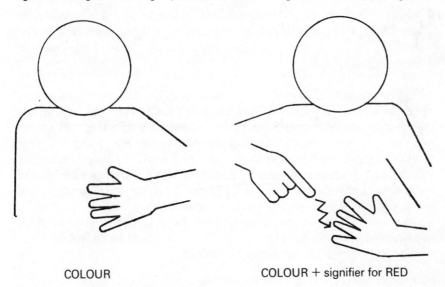

COLOUR   COLOUR + signifier for RED

The mime element of the system can be seen in the sign BLOOD, which suggests the liquid trickling downwards.

The principle of conceptual grouping helps intellectually able adults to learn and remember the signs. Proponents of PGSS suggest that although children are not taught to analyse signs into their component features (e.g. COLOUR + BLOOD = RED), nevertheless their concept development is helped by the patterns in the system. This may well be the case, though research evidence is not yet available.

Markers in the form of arbitrary signs allow the grammatical features of English to be reflected. These plus the one-to-one sign-to-word correspondence make the system sufficiently detailed for written English to be 'signed aloud'. However, Craig (1978) suggests that just as some spoken English is very simple or even ungrammatical, so PGSS can be simplified to the point where root forms only are used by severely handicapped people.

The first experimental teaching of PGSS to deaf people, the population for whom it was originally devised, took place in 1964 and it is still more widely used with deaf and deaf-blind children than with any others. Even so, Rowe (1978), speaking from her experience with many severely mentally and physically handicapped children, believes that the system can be quite appropriate for this other population, given correctly structured teaching methods. As with other signing systems, it is said that the simultaneous use of speech alongside the signs, allied with a Total Communication approach, makes a vital contribution to its meaningfulness.

Discussion Point 1:

> '*Because PGSS is based on English language structures, it offers mentally handicapped clients (as well as the deaf population for whom it was devised) an especially good foundation for the later development of grammatical speech.*'

On logical grounds, this comment appears to be legitimate, though unsupported by research evidence (Kiernan, Reid and Jones 1982). However, as with SE, the full grammatical complexity of PGSS as used when reflecting adult speech may be too great for mentally handicapped clients (though see Rowe (1978) as mentioned above and Fenn and Rowe (1975)). The use of a simplified form of PGSS may still act as a stimulus to speech because it encourages the habit of communication, but in this case the foundation for speech development would not be provided by 'English language structures'.

Since other signing systems may similarly be simplified to suit a mentally handicapped client, other bases of comparison should be looked at when considering the possible advantages of PGSS.

Figure 2.12: Paget Gorman Sign System Iconic Sign

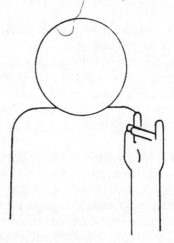

ANIMAL

Discussion Point 2:

> '*The pantomimic signs of PGSS are easily understood.*'

PGSS was devised with the intention that it should be largely pantomimic, i.e. that the signs should be representational in mimed form. It is true that many signs are reasonably iconic, for example ANIMAL in Figure 2.12, in which the ears and muzzle of an animal can be distinguished. Understanding the representational nature of other signs demands quite a high level of knowledge, as can be seen from the example in Figure 2.13. To suggest that YEAR is representational assumes a knowledge of the earth's rotation round the sun. Other signs are representational only in part or somewhat remotely. For example, in the sign RED (Figure 2.11) the meaning as a whole could not be understood without a previous knowledge that the spread hand signified COLOUR and of course red blood is not the only liquid that trickles downwards. A naive observer would be unlikely to deduce the meaning of the sign RED.

Figure 2.13: Paget Gorman Sign System Sign with Underlying Iconicity

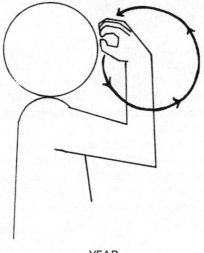

YEAR

'Easily' in the initial comment is a relative term. The transparency or guessability of PGSS is not an outstanding characteristic overall, even though at an intellectual level it is possible to trace the representational basis of the signs.

Discussion Point 3:

'PGSS is inappropriate for people with a physical handicap owing to the difficulty and complexity of its sign formation.'

Many of the standard hand postures and basic signs require very specific finger positions and the range of movement in the arms is precisely specified. Furthermore, PGSS includes a relatively high percentage of two-handed constructions (Kiernan, Jordan and Saunders 1978). It is therefore often considered that two good hands capable of fine finger movements are required in order to use PGSS. This is certainly the case if accuracy is at a premium, but at least one large school whose pupils are severely physically as well as mentally handicapped has successfully established the use of PGSS. If, as in spoken communication, approximations are acceptable provided they can be understood, then a potentially quite wide range of physically handicapped people can communicate by means of PGSS and, for example, some individuals with the use of only one hand can sign two-handed items in sequence instead of simultaneously. Of course if the individual's *mental* disability is also severe, this very practical but cognitively demanding solution to the problem may be beyond him.

Discussion Point 4:

   'PGSS benefits from a sophisticated organisation for training teachers and maintaining standards.'

The system for training and examining professional who wish to learn PGSS and implement its use is certainly quite elaborate. Five-day residential workshops or series of weekly lessons are conducted by highly trained personnel. The standard of signing technique is maintained through only awarding the PGSS certificate and diploma for genuine competence in those who have received tuition.

   It could, however, be argued that these demands are rather formidable for people who do not want their abilities to be minutely scrutinised. It is possible that such high standards may make PGSS less acceptable to establishments wishing to set up signing on a trial basis, whose staff cannot or do not wish to meet the training standards that are required by the PGSS organisation.

Finger Spelling

Finger spelling is a signed representation of the alphabet. One sign stands for one letter and no grammatical construction is involved.

   Although the written alphabet remains virtually the same across many languages and in different English-speaking countries, the manual alphabets are distinctly different. Some, like the American manual alphabet, are performed with one hand only. Others, including the British, require two hands (see Discussion Point 2 below). As can be seen from the selection of letters in Figure 2.14, the signs may approximate to the written letters. The finger-spelled D, for example, resembles the lower-case letter in American and the upper-case letter in the British alphabet.

   Finger spelling can be used in isolation, in which case the user must possess a basic ability to spell. However, such use is unusual and cumbersome and finger spelling is more commonly employed in combination with another communication system. The Rochester Method, for example, used by some deaf people in North America, accompanies speech by finger spelling and a

Figure 2.14: Signs from American and British Manual Alphabets

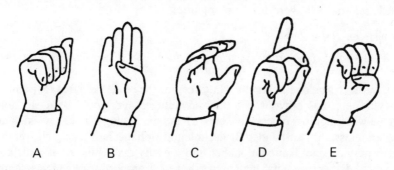

American manual alphabet (Used with permission from Gallaudet College Press)

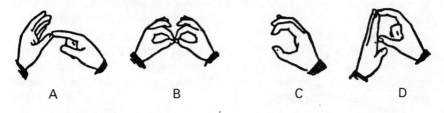

British manual alphabet

similar technique is promoted in the Soviet Union. Most often, it is used by intelligent deaf signers to extend their main signing system, e.g. BSL or SE, especially to spell out a technical or unfamiliar word and to express proper names in terms of their initials. Total Communication as a philosophy also admits finger spelling as required by the user.

Finger spelling is an entirely abstract form of signing; the letters which some signs resemble are themselves abstract. Discussion Point 3 below considers whether, as such, it is relevant to the needs of mentally handicapped people.

Discussion Point 1:

   'The manual alphabet and its use for finger spelling are easy to learn.'

An intelligent adult could probably learn the letter-signs with half an hour or so of tuition and with the 26 letters of the English alphabet a whole language can potentially be expressed.

However, learning to use finger spelling fluidly is very much less easy, and following the expression of an experienced finger speller requires great skill and practice. (To get even a slight inkling of the difficulty, try understanding a few sentences read out at speed letter by letter.) As with Morse code, a receiver eventually learns to anticipate and confirm the content of the message without analysing its individual letters, a technique not wholly dissimilar from conventional reading, though probably depending more heavily on the first and last letters of each word for its recognition.

Discussion Point 2:

  'A one-handed alphabet is more practical than a two-handed alphabet.'

Being able to sign one-handedly while keeping the other hand free for pointing, carrying, etc. has obvious practical advantages and would be easier for a person with impaired functioning of one hand or needing to hold a walking aid. Nevertheless, the two-handed British manual alphabet is arguably clearer than the American one-handed alphabet, more easily distinguished at a distance and more distinctive in its sign-shapes, a greater proportion of which resemble the written letters. Its finger positions are more naturally assumed and probably require less physical dexterity. Moreover, the advantages of a one-handed alphabet are minimised if it is being used in conjunction with another two-handed signing system.

   However, the over-riding consideration is that when in Rome one should do as the Romans do. In other words, since above all it is important that the finger spelling should be understood, in the USA the American alphabet is the one to use, and in the UK the British.

Discussion Point 3:

  'Finger spelling is inappropriate for mentally handicapped people.'

Though an ability to spell might be thought essential in order to use finger spelling, this is not quite the case. Most signing systems that have been adapted for mentally handicapped people incorporate minor elements of finger spelling. Even the Makaton Vocabulary, compiled specifically for this population, for TELEVISION spells out TV using the British manual alphabet, and MOTHER is a twice-repeated M. Mentally handicapped individuals can also be taught to sign initial letters for people's names.

   However, such uses as these of the manual alphabet cannot really be described as 'spelling'; it is probable that mentally handicapped users do not differentiate the letter-signs from other more conceptually related signs. The level of understanding of conventional spelling necessary to use, say, the Rochester Method would be well beyond the cognitive reach of this population.

A Comparison between Signing Systems

When comparing signing systems, it is necessary to think in terms of the target population and its particular needs. What is relevant or even an especial priority in one context is not always universally so. The present target population is, of course, mentally handicapped people; five aspects of the systems have been singled out for comparison.

Transparency of Signs

When the meaning of signs is obvious, they are easier to learn. Because the meaning of iconic signs and those based on natural gesture is easier to guess than the meaning of abstract or arbitrary signs, they are likely to facilitate learning. This is naturally an advantage for severely mentally handicapped clients.

Research indicates that half or more of the total number of Amer-Ind signals can be understood by an uninstructed observer, which is a significantly higher proportion than in other systems. Although PGSS signs are based on mime, their iconicity is often obscure; recognition of it may depend on previous knowledge or on associations which are quite cognitively demanding. Many BSL signs have iconic features, especially those representing simple everyday concepts. However, as can be gathered from the examples in Figure 2.8, the iconic association is often outdated, making such signs appear arbitrary.

Ease of Execution

As may be expected, when signs are easy to perform clients tend to use them more willingly. Conversely, signs which are difficult to perform may be a deterrent to communication, especially if motivation is in any case quite low. Ease of execution is determined by three factors: handshape, whether one or both hands are used and, if both, whether they are used symmetrically or asymmetrically.

Handshape. The easiest handshapes to assume are those which are natural, such as an open flat hand, a fist or a pointing index finger. Handshapes of this type, with few exceptions, are used in BSL (and its derivatives) and Amer-Ind. The most physically demanding system is PGSS with the largest number of handshapes in regular use, some quite difficult to assume without practice.

Use of One or Both Hands. Clients with only one fully functional hand will naturally cope better with one-handed signs. The use of only one hand may also be easier for clients with limited mental ability.

About half the total vocabulary of Amer-Ind is made up of one-handed signals and one-handed adaptations of the remainder have been devised by Skelly. Within a similar vocabulary range, BSL and its derivatives have a lower proportion of one-handed signs and PGSS has only a few.

Symmetrical or Asymmetrical Signs. Symmetrical signs, i.e. those in which both hands take up the same position and (where this is involved) carry out the same movement, are easier to learn because they make lower cognitive demands than two-hands-different signs. Once they have been learnt, their performance is also physically easier.

Most two-handed Amer-Ind signals and many BSL signs are executed with both hands in symmetrical positions, whereas the majority of PGSS signs are performed with two hands in different positions.

Available Vocabulary

Although many mentally handicapped clients will not acquire a large vocabulary, it is important that what is available should answer needs. The vocabulary requirements of a particular setting, for example the educational demands of the classroom, are also relevant.

The number of BSL signs (like the words in a spoken language) is expanding all the time. All are also acceptable in SE, though the UK SE handbooks will only contain a core of about 1500 items – which is likely to be sufficient for most mentally handicapped people. The PGSS vocabulary in the complete manual includes over double that number and more items are officially issued from time to time. These systems can be expected to include most of the 'special interest' signs that might be required by individuals. The limited vocabulary of Amer-Ind can if necessary be extended by agglutinations, though attaching multiple signs to a single concept may be somewhat demanding for mentally handicapped people. The fundamental principles of the Makaton Vocabulary depend on its limited vocabulary; this may or may not fit the requirements of a particular client.

Flexibility of Expression

The chosen system should be adequate for whatever messages clients need or may wish to convey, ranging from the very simple to the much more complex, including the progression from one to the other.

At a basic level, the Makaton Vocabulary may serve quite adequately to answer needs, but nuances of expression are beyond its range. Straightforward communication is available within Amer-Ind's broad concepts and the agglutination technique permits some flexibility and more specific expression. The limitations on precision that do exist may not be felt as restrictive by many mentally handicapped clients. The range of expression of PGSS, SE and BSL is similar to that of the spoken language. However, though the first two can be equally precise, as contrived systems they lack the flexibility of the natural language, BSL.

Of course flexibility and a wide expressive range comprise only one aspect of several to consider when choosing a system and their relevance for different individuals will vary.

Support for Speech

The degree of direct support that a signing system offers to speech depends on the degree of correspondence between them. However, it seems likely that a more general communicative support should not be ruled out.

As an independent language, BSL is remote from English in its form of expression. Longer 'utterances' of Amer-Ind may also be remote owing to the economical use of signals in unspecified order; on the other hand, very simple Amer-Ind utterances may quite closely reflect the number and order of words in a spoken utterance. Whatever the level of utterance, Skelly states that the able person should accompany signing with speech, the signals slightly preceding the spoken words. An able person is also recommended to accompany the Makaton Vocabulary with full grammatical speech; direct support of speech will be limited to key words, which should be signed simultaneously as they are spoken. The precise sign-to-word correspondence of SE and PGSS can reflect and so provide direct support for any level of spoken English, which, it is recommended, should be used simultaneously.

Use of every one of the systems has been shown to stimulate and facilitate the initiation and use of speech. It may be that, in the early stages at least, simple practice of another form of communication is the chief elicitor of speech, more influential than any particular relation of a sign system to English.

A summary of the points raised above appears in Figure 2.15. We must emphasise again that the 'best buy' is dependent on individual needs and priorities.

Figure 2.15: Characteristics of Five Signing Systems

	Amer-Ind	BSL	Signed English	Makaton Vocabulary	PGSS
Transparency	+				
Easy handshapes	+	+	+	+	−
Use of one hand only	+				−
Both hands symmetrical	+				−
Wide available vocabulary		+	+		+
Relation to speech order		−	+	+	+
Relation to grammar of speech		−	−	+	−	+

3   SYMBOLS AND SYMBOL SYSTEMS

The word 'symbol' can be used with a variety of related but different meanings, which have already been referred to in Chapter 1. However, for the sake of clarity, at the beginning of a chapter entitled 'Symbols' we will define the term more fully. We will then look at the development of symbol systems for communication. The major part of the chapter will describe and discuss individual systems, after which there will be a brief comparison of different aspects of the systems.

Symbols and Symbolic Thought

The first awareness of a child is concerned with his bodily sensations and the world around him is entirely perceived through his senses. Gradually his awareness extends to the realisation that much of what he perceives is related to or stands for something else. For example, the sound that he hears of a spoon against a plate, or the sight of a spoon being placed on the table in front of him, comes to signify food. A child recognising this relationship is engaged in early symbolic thought, the sound of the spoon or the spoon itself being the symbol for food. As symbolic thought advances, the symbol can still be recognised as standing for something else when it is less concretely related to it – for example, a two-dimensional picture of a spoon can be recognised as standing for a real spoon or even, in certain circumstances, for food.

Development of symbolic thought is associated with concept acquisition. A concept has been acquired when a child's sensory perceptions (and eventually his abstract ideas) are mentally organised so that their relationships can be appreciated. For example, the concept 'cup' has been acquired when the child can generalise from a picture of a specific cup to seeing that it is related to different cups, both in pictures and as real objects. In acquiring the concept the child must also realise that, say, a bowl or a bottle are *not* cups.

Concepts can have linguistic symbols, i.e. words, attached to them, so that, for example, the word 'cup' stands for all kinds of cups. Words, which are themselves abstract, can stand either for something concrete (e.g. a cup or Peter) or for something abstract (e.g. day, hurry, boredom, pleasant). These words/concepts can be represented by various sorts of symbol, such as a manual sign, a series of letters (i.e. a written word), a representational picture, a more or less abstract drawing, a cut-out shape and so on.

All the above are symbols, but the 'symbols' which form the central subject-matter of this chapter are the sets which have been gathered together to make up communication systems. In particular, these are written or drawn symbols, i.e. graphic symbols, and two-dimensional cut-out shapes. For convenience, both types are usually referred to simply as 'symbols', though a distinction may be made between graphic symbols and symbol shapes.

Symbol Systems for Communication

Symbol systems date back to ancient times. The Ancient Egyptians, for example, developed the system of picture-writing we know as hieroglyphics and other early systems were probably pictographic. In these, words were represented by single symbols which were not so much pictures as highly stylised drawings, sometimes referred to as logographs. The majority were quite easily decipherable because they directly resembled what they represented. Words which could not be easily and concretely represented utilised the 'rebus principle'. According to this principle, one pictograph can represent all words which sound the same, so that, for example, ORE, OR and OAR can all be punningly represented by a picture of an oar. Alternatively, different pictographs can be employed to represent each syllable of a word, so that, for example, 'belief' becomes BEE + LEAF.

To overcome problems of representation and of learning enormous numbers of symbols (as in hieroglyphics), most logographic systems gradually evolved to syllabic as opposed to whole-word representation. This reduced the memory load for people learning the system, but at the same time made decoding more complex, because although the total number of symbols in use was smaller, they were no longer conceptually related to the words. The relationship was through sound and so the meaning was a step away.

Symbol sets were still further reduced in size with the emergence of alphabets; thus the efficiency of writing increased because relatively few symbols were needed to represent the sound units of words. However, the task became harder still for a beginner in reading, as alphabets are probably the most difficult type of system to learn owing to the number of units which must be processed within any single word.

In recent times, easy decodability has become especially important for some purposes and populations, so where the need has arisen non-alphabetic systems have been preferred. Those presently in use share some of the features of the old logographic and syllabic systems.

Symbols for Handicapped People

A characteristic of manual sign language such as BSL and ASL is their evolution over time, which contrasts with the origin of contrived systems. Among symbol systems we find none that have evolved naturally for a population with a specific handicap, though some have been devised for this purpose. Braille, for example, is an alphabetic system for blind people which replaces letters with raised dots. It was invented in 1829 by a Frenchman called Louis Braille, himself blind from the age of three.

Symbol systems in use with mentally handicapped people have mostly been devised for other purposes. Of the systems described in the present chapter, Blissymbols, Rebus, developments of Premack's symbol shapes and Worldsign all fall into this category. The Sigsymbol system was designed as a teaching tool for severely mentally handicapped children. To assist comparisons, the communicative use of pictures and of the conventional alphabet are also discussed briefly.

Rarely will a severely mentally handicapped person who communicates through graphic symbols be able to draw them himself. For the majority, expression will be by means of one of two techniques: either the 'transmitter' will be presented with an array of symbols to which he must point one at a time, or the array will consist of individual symbol units which the transmitter has to pick up and place in position to formulate his message.

Some clients with an associated physical handicap will have so little use of their hands that even pointing with a finger will be beyond them. They may be able to gain access to a symbol system through technical aids, a number of which are described in Chapter 4. Some of these may also help to motivate profoundly mentally handicapped clients.

The format of the rest of this chapter follows that of Chapter 2. After the description of each system, certain issues will be raised under the heading of 'discussion points'.

Picture Communication

A long-standing but formally undeveloped non-speech method of communicating is through pictures, with varying amounts of detail, either drawings or photographs.

Some advantages of photographs are obvious. They can give the closest possible two-dimensional representation of a three-dimensional object, so helping a mentally handicapped person to appreciate the correspondence between the two. Photographs of views and places will provide an evident likeness of the original, and the client himself can appear in the photograph – a great attraction to those who are able to recognise themselves, which may trigger memories and motivate an attempt to communicate. Expertise is not necessary to produce clear, recognisable photographs and, with an instant camera, on-the-spot reproduction is possible.

Drawings have the advantage of being able to highlight particular features and an object can be made to stand out sharply from its background; indeed, no background at all need be included (nor need there be in a cut-out photograph). However, without doubt more skill is needed to produce good, clear, attractive drawings than to take photographs.

It is possible to see the two types of picture as part of a continuum leading to more abstract symbols. Photographs may be the simplest introduction to two-dimensional representation as they most clearly resemble the original. These can be followed by detailed representational drawings, followed by more stylised drawings, followed by impressionistic sketches or simplified line drawings.

Such a sequenced and logical progression is not always necessary for understanding. The authors know one boy in his late teens who had learned to match photographs with each other and line drawings with each other but could not cross-match nor relate them to the real object. In one memorable teaching session he suddenly grasped the equivalence of a toy telephone and a photograph of it. Immediately he went on to demonstrate that he could match a black-and-white line drawing with either the object or the photograph. In this instance the *degree* of likeness proved to be unimportant; the critical factor was an understanding of the relationship between two and three dimensions.

As with all symbols, when pictures are being used as a day-to-day communication method they need to be adequately displayed. Display can be arranged on a portable board, the number, size and arrangement being varied to suit the client. Alternative methods are suggested in Chapter 4.

Drawings and photographs can also be used as a teaching aid, for example in matching and sorting exercises, in specific language programmes (e.g. for teaching opposites or positional prepositions), or as a general stimulus to communication, possibly in conjunction with other non-speech techniques.

Discussion Point 1:

'Pictures are an excellent non-speech aid because they can be readily interpreted by a handicapped person and by the rest of the community.'

In itself a picture may be perfectly clear, but this does not mean it can always convey an unambiguous message. A client who points at the picture of a washbasin may mean that he wants to wash his hands or that he has just done so. Pointing at a photograph of a girl eating a meal could be interpreted as 'girl', 'dinner', 'fish and chips', 'I'm hungry' or even 'That girl looks like my sister.' Obviously the context of time and place helps, as does the body language of the client, but the precise meaning may still be difficult to interpret.

As a vocabulary of pictures accumulates, so a convention for interpreting them needs to be established. The convention might include formalising the pictures so that they come to resemble pictographic Rebus symbols or Sigsymbols (see sections later in this chapter).

Some professionals may feel that, as a permanent communication method, pictures are insufficiently precise or consistent. Staff in an establishment may also prefer a more standardised system, as one aspect of a secure and predictable environment.

Discussion Point 2:

 'Pictures have limitations in providing a medium for language development.'

Pictures can contribute to concept development. The picture of a biscuit associated with, say, a plateful of a whole variety of different biscuits may help a client to generalise the concept of a biscuit beyond those which resemble the one in the picture.

However, pictures cannot truly represent abstract concepts, though some may attempt to do so through specifying the context, e.g. a picture of someone being given a particular item might be used to represent the abstract concept 'give'. Nor do pictures reflect the grammatical structures of language, either the inflections (-ing, -ed, etc.) or the function words ('the', 'what?', 'may', etc.). These are certainly limiting factors to the usefulness of pictures as the sole medium for promoting language development, though they may be helpful stimuli in combination with other more strictly linguistic systems.

Symbol Shapes

During the late 1960s and early 1970s, several research studies on primates were conducted with the aim of determining their ability to use language through a medium other than speech. Notable among these was the Premacks' pioneering work with a chimpanzee called Sarah (Premack 1970; Premack and Premack 1972). Sarah was taught using arbitrarily shaped flat pieces of plastic in place of words. (Iconicity was avoided in order to determine her ability to handle abstract language.) Her correct responses were shaped and reinforced by a structured schedule of rewards so that she learned to discriminate shapes, associate meanings with them and respond to questions.

Non-SLIP

Inspired by Premack's success, Carrier and Peak (1975) devised a scheme for initiating language development in profoundly handicapped children. Known as 'Non-SLIP', which stands for 'Non-Speech Language Initiation Program', the procedures teach on the one hand discrimination of shapes and the association of meaning (picture labelling) and on the other the building of a grammatically correct seven-word sentence. The sentence is constructed according to the pattern 'The (noun) is (verb)ing (preposition) the (noun)', e.g. 'The boy is sitting in the car.'

The Non-SLIP symbols, 30 in number, are made of white plastic, the actual choice of shapes differing from Premack's but remaining non-representational. The symbol-shapes are colour-coded to indicate their position in the sentence. Clients are taught to arrange them in a left-to-right sequence on a display board with seven slots. At first, placing depends solely on colour coding. Later, when clients have also learned to label simple pictures with single symbols (first nouns, then verbs and prepositions), the whole sentence is constructed in meaningful grammatical response to a picture.

Before following the main Non-SLIP programme, clients must have achieved certain prerequisite skills. These include attention to the task, appropriate use of the hands (picking up and placing), and colour matching. Supplementary procedures are laid down in the programme for teaching these skills. This and all other parts of Non-SLIP are tightly structured along behavioural lines: tasks are broken down into very small steps, rewards are selected to reinforce learning and charts of the procedures are provided for detailed recording of results.

Non-SLIP is not immediately concerned with 'real-life' situations. A client learns a particular syntactic structure rather than broader-based communication skills and the vocabulary is unrelated to everyday needs. (For example, one illustration requiring a full-sentence response shows a cow sitting on a car.) However, it is not intended as a communication *system*, nor does it aim to provide a comprehensive training programme; its aim is the initiation of language. Carrier and Peak suggest that children who have followed the programme successfully, many of whom start to vocalise spontaneously during training sessions, may be ready to proceed to other more conventional programmes, e.g. for speech training.

The Deich and Hodges System

Premack's work with primates also served as the starting point for Deich and Hodges' research into the use of symbols. This is outlined in their book *Language Without Speech* (Deich and Hodges 1977). As in Non-SLIP, plastic symbols are used, though these differ in shape both from the Non-SLIP symbols and Premack's in that some – seemingly chosen at random – are vaguely iconic, while the remainder are arbitrary. Examples can be seen in Figure 3.1. Symbols, about a hundred in number, are colour coded according to speech functions. A systematic teaching procedure is described, to be carried out according to behavioural principles.

Children are first taught to associate and distinguish between symbol and real object. Initially, the correct placing of a symbol on a tray is rewarded by whatever the symbol represents; for example, correct choice of the apple symbol is rewarded by a piece of apple. Later, edible rewards are dropped in favour of social rewards. Many individual symbols are learned before selection from an array of symbols is required. Deich and Hodges stress their use of errorless learning, achieved through the teacher's guiding the child's hand as necessary.

In contrast to the Non-SLIP programme, there is no attempt to teach a relatively complex sentence structure. The symbols are, however, arranged from left to right on a flat tray, with a gradual progression from single words to

Figure 3.1: Symbols from the Deich and Hodges System

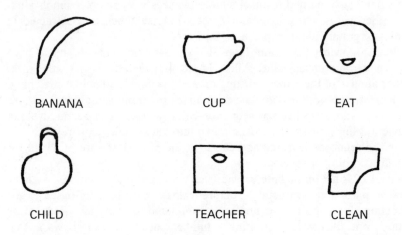

two words, and so on. This represents a closer relation to normal language development than does Non-SLIP.

Another feature of the Deich and Hodges teaching procedures demand practical responses such as eating and cleaning, and relate to a real communicative exchange. The authors believe that the manipulation of objects is an important sensory input for the low-functioning children who follow the programme. As with Non-SLIP, they believe that using the system acts as a facilitator for speech and/or signing and increases children's responsiveness and readiness to interact socially.

Discussion Point 1:

   'The Non-SLIP and Deich and Hodges materials are expensive and difficult to obtain.'

The Non-SLIP package of symbols, display board, manual and record sheets is obtainable through an American supplier, H & H Enterprises, Kansas City, Kansas. It is, however, very expensive and its purchase could not be undertaken lightly by any educational establishment. No source is known to the present authors for commercially obtaining the Deich and Hodges materials. However, their book, *Language Without Speech* describes the programme and includes an appendix which gives samples of symbol shapes. Without infringement of copyright, similar step-by-step language programmes could be individually designed. Additional symbol-shapes, either iconic or arbitrary, could also be designed and constructed out of plastic, wood, card, etc.

Discussion Point 2:

   'Most of the symbol-shapes that were used in the programmes described were arbitrary. This is unlikely to assist the learning process.'

While published accounts suggest that learning is quite rapid, this may simply result from the well-organised framework of learning. In our opinion, there is no advantage to arbitrary and abstract shapes when it is generally recognised that iconicity assists learning and retention. Premack's wish to prove that primates could use functional language of an arbitrary nature is not relevant in the context of mentally handicapped children, whose need is for improved communication. It is worth noting that the second set of symbols designed by Deich and Hodges contains a number of items that have been redesigned with iconic features.

Nevertheless, despite the limitations of symbol design, the Non-SLIP and Deich and Hodges procedures have much to offer anyone who is interested in non-speech alternatives. Their special strength is that instead of, as with many alternative systems, concentrating on the nature and quality of the expressive medium, the authors have wholeheartedly devoted their energies to developing detailed and effective teaching programmes.

Discussion Point 3:

 'Programmes involving symbol-shapes are an unsatisfactory way of developing broad communication skills.'

Reports from the authors of the two systems described give quite optimistic accounts of the progress of individuals who previously had little or no language. It seems likely that such progress was dependent on the structured programmes which were undertaken in a one-to-one situation. Once a basic level of language has been acquired, other programmes and settings may become more appropriate to give broader opportunities for the practice of communication. The change may be desirable for several reasons. Firstly, since intensive programmes make heavy demands on everyday classroom teaching schedules, group teaching is preferable if it is effective. Secondly (especially in the case of Non-SLIP), after formal language initiation, freer and more natural communication can be achieved using a variety of less formal structures. Thirdly, the group provides a natural setting for the social interaction which can motivate communication.

Discussion Point 4:

 'Systems of symbol-shapes are troublesome for practical day-to-day communication.'

The need to carry round a tray plus a particular selection of symbols naturally limits the usefulness of these systems for impromptu conversation. Symbols lying loose on a tray are easily dropped (or thrown) and the selection can quickly become a confused jumble or even be scattered and lost. Clients with athetoid cerebral palsy (who involuntarily twist and writhe) may find it even more difficult to place a symbol precisely than to produce approximate versions of signs.

It would in fact be true to say that symbol-shape systems are troublesome to use in practical day-to-day communication. However, before condemning them out of hand for such shortcomings, the *aim* of these systems should be remembered, i.e. language initiation.

Blissymbolics

Blissymbols owe their creation to Charles Bliss, an Austrian Jew born in 1897. As a young man he was strongly aware of the communication in his own land where many different languages were spoken and was an enthusiastic supporter of Esperanto and its ideals. During the Second World War he was imprisoned and then escaped to China where he became interested in their picture-writing. In his previous work as a research chemist, he had used standardised formulae to communicate scientific ideas across language barriers. His belief, arising from these experiences, was that an international symbol system would minimise misunderstandings between different cultures and nations and so promote world peace.

The system that he devised, which he called Semantography (i.e. 'meaning-writing'), kindled no immediate enthusiasm or demand, but Bliss eventually published a book entitled *Semantography* (Bliss 1965). In 1971, Shirley McNaughton of the Ontario Crippled Children's Centre in Toronto, Canada, came across Bliss's work while searching for a communication system for use with the non-verbal physically handicapped children she was teaching. Since then, the system, under its new name of Blissymbolics, has emerged as one of the most important international developments in special education, achieving some of its originator's ideals in a manner he never initially envisaged.

The symbols are related to meanings and ideas, falling into four different categories: (1) very simplified representational pictographs, as illustrated in Figure 3.2; (2) simple ideographs relating to an idea, as illustrated in Figure 3.3; (3) arbitrary symbols, as illustrated in Figure 3.4; (4) internationally recognised symbols, as illustrated in Figure 3.5.

Figure 3.2: Bliss Pictographic Symbols

HOUSE   TREE   MAN   ANIMAL

The most common method of use is for the symbols to be displayed on a communication board to be pointed at and read by users and 'listeners'. Symbols are arranged in a grid, the number that appear being dependent on the

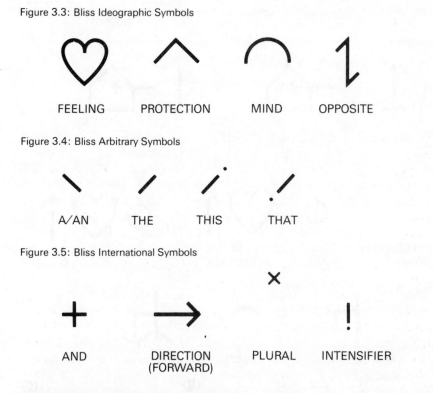

Figure 3.3: Bliss Ideographic Symbols

FEELING   PROTECTION   MIND   OPPOSITE

Figure 3.4: Bliss Arbitrary Symbols

A/AN   THE   THIS   THAT

Figure 3.5: Bliss International Symbols

AND   DIRECTION   PLURAL   INTENSIFIER
       (FORWARD)

ability of the user. The upper limit is dictated by the practicalities of size and clarity and is normally no more than 400 symbols. Word categories may be grouped and colour-coded for quick selection.

This limited number of symbols can be enlarged by the use of indicators and strategies making it possible to express an infinite number of new ideas. Indicators specify the part of speech or the tense of a verb which is represented by the symbol. The strategies include the 'combine' strategy, which enables the user to choose an *ad hoc* series of symbols to represent a new meaning. As some Blissymbols represent a concept rather than a precise word, they have a range of meaning and can be given a number of synonyms. For example, one symbol-combine might mean PRETTY, HANDSOME, ATTRACTIVE, PLEASING etc. In a whole sentence combines are enclosed within 'combine indicators', so as not to become confused with the rest of the sentence structure (e.g. see ELEPHANT Figure 3.6). In contrast 'compound' symbols are multicharacter items which are fully incorporated by the Blissymbolics Communication Institute as part of the Standard Bliss Vocabulary (e.g. see VISITOR, ATTRACTIVE and TOILET Figure 3.6).

Combines, as expressed by a sophisticated Bliss user, are virtually an art form, and the flexibility of the symbols is only limited by the creativity of the user. This creativity contrasts with the very precise rules laid down for

Figure 3.6: Bliss 'Compound' and 'Combination' Symbols

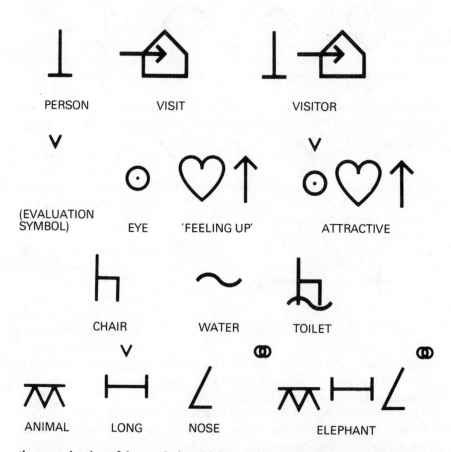

the reproduction of the symbols, which apply to correct spacing and exactness of drawing to ensure correct size and positioning. These are determined with reference to a square located between 'earthline' and 'skyline'. The rules are important because symbol meanings may change according to size and position (see Figure 3.7).

Figure 3.7: Blissymbols Drawn Relative to Earthline and Skyline

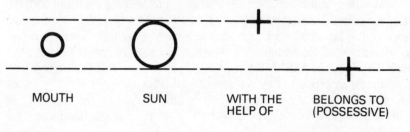

Blissymbols may be structured in a way that directly reflects English grammar, which in practice is often simplified to telegraphic form for the convenience of handicapped people. Alternatively, there are syntactic (grammatical) rules laid down by Bliss, which he claims represent a more universal format independent of the structure of a specific language. Those who are experienced in the use of the system suggest that it needs to be viewed as an independent visual communication system, with natural syntactic structure that differs from spoken language forms.

The most widespread use of Bliss has been with physically handicapped people with normal or near-normal intellectual ability. Clients use finger-pointing to indicate symbols if their physical state permits this. Otherwise eye-pointing may be used or – following a considerable amount of research – various aids have been developed to extend communication possibilities. These include electro-mechanical and electronic aids, computer representation of the symbols and simulated speech. Some of these are described in Chapter 4.

The more complicated methods of indicating a symbol, such as by number-coding its position on a grid, require quite a high level of cognitive ability, especially when the 400-symbol chart is involved. However, relatively small Bliss vocabularies have been used successfully with mentally handicapped people who show a desire to communicate and can demonstrate other prerequisites for starting on a programme; these include an ability to indicate yes and no, to differentiate size, shape and direction, and to relate to black-and-white pictures. Difficulties of discriminating between symbols may be eased by colour-coding. Another aid to discrimination is pictorial enhancement of the symbols. This approach is described and some 300 enhanced symbols illustrated in *Picture Your Blissymbols* (BCI 1985); the complete kit also contains a manual and teaching materials.

Recently, some programmes have been devised for parallel tuition in Blissymbols and the Makaton Vocabulary (outlined in Chapter 2), which may assist people with varying degrees of handicap to work together. Blissymbols are also used to develop and assess reading skills. Not only do the symbols give practice and experience in a number of pre-reading skills, but at a later stage they can act as a substitute for speech in reading 'aloud'.

In the early 1970s, the Blissymbolics Communication Foundation – now known as the Blissymbolics Communication Institute – was set up in Toronto, having as its aim the development of Blissymbols for use by handicapped people. Following this, a system of qualifying courses for instructors has been established. Qualified British instructors/lecturers are based at the Blissymbolics Resource Centre (UK) in Cardiff, Wales and can provide information about the system and courses. Many centres in the UK have come to use Bliss since it was introduced in 1974.

Materials available include *Teaching Guidelines* (McNaughton, Kates and Silverman 1975), *Teaching and Using Blissymbolics* (McDonald 1980), a symbol dictionary (Hehner 1980), symbol charts and templates for drawing symbols. There is also a compendious *Handbook of Blissymbolics* (Silverman, McNaughton and Kates 1978), which details a wide range of information about many aspects of the system as well as numerous teaching strategies and aids.

Discussion Point 1:

> *'Bliss is unsuitable for use by mentally handicapped people because many of the symbols require fine discrimination.'*

It is true that many symbols require fine discrimination. They are constructed from a small number of basic geometric shapes and, as illustrated in Figure 3.7 above, according to the size and position of some symbols their meaning may change. The orientation of an arrow determines its meaning, and, while a small V-shape over a word indicates an adjective or adverb, if the shape is inverted it indicates a verb. Many other examples items could be added.

Some mentally handicapped people have problems in visual perception, experiencing difficulties in making sense of what they see, even when relatively gross discrimination is required. Certain strategies may be helpful, as well as the conventional one of enlarging the size of the symbols as a set. One possibility is to emphasise the most meaningful part of the symbol using a thicker pen or a different colour, or pictorially embellish some individual symbols (cf. the discussion of symbol elaboration in the section entitled 'Alphabetic Script' later in this chapter).

The Bliss authorities acknowledge that the symbols may present difficulties for some people and make it clear that the system is not the answer for every non-speaking person. Other less perceptually demanding systems may be more appropriate.

Discussion Point 2:

> *'The complexities of the Blissymbol System are too great for the intellectual development of mentally handicapped people.'*

This is a more fundamental point than Discussion Point 1, for it refers to the client's understanding of the system and not simply his visual perception of it. In effect, it questions whether the system can be meaningful to a mentally handicapped person.

Some Blissymbols, for example those illustrated in Figure 3.2, are reasonably pictographic. However, there are certainly complexities in the system, both in terms of abstract markers and the conceptually compiled combination symbols (as in Figure 3.6). Nevertheless, some mentally handicapped people may in any case be perceiving some representational items as arbitrary – rather like reading by the look-and-say method without analysing the sound-values of the letters. To people using this approach, many aspects of the underlying conceptual reasoning are superfluous, perhaps even distracting. Some clients, on the other hand, may be capable of learning about the conceptually related aspects by following a structured programme.

Another complexity in the conventional way of using Blissymbols is that sentences and 'combination' symbols require sequenced pointing for their expression, which makes considerable demands on short-term memory, quite apart from the conceptual grasp and creativity needed to devise them in the first place. Some methods of display may help to overcome this difficulty. The *Handbook of Blissymbolics* (Silverman *et al.* 1978) suggests among other devices a kind of abacus with sliding symbols which can be arranged at leisure for semi-permanent display and a symbol pegboard with spare holes on the front row for constructing sentences.

Whether the intellectual demands of the Blissymbol system can be met by a mentally handicapped client can only be decided on an individual basis, possibly after a period of experimentation.

Discussion Point 3:

> *'If a mentally handicapped person is sufficiently able to learn Blissymbolics, it would be better to concentrate on teaching him to read words instead.'*

The first Blissymbols to be taught are simple pictographs which relate directly to meaning. In contrast, when the first spelled words are learned there is no meaning-relationship to assist; instead, abstract letters must be related to sounds and word-recognition is dependent on entirely abstract shapes. This places heavier demands on memory than picture recognition, even when the pictographic nature of symbols is very much simplified, as for example, in some Blissymbols. However, even abstract Blissymbols are usually more distinctive than different letters of the alphabet; moreover they can be directly decoded into meaningful words rather than into sounds bearing no meaning of their own.

Both symbols and words can, however, provide a vehicle for communication. The initial use of Bliss gives experience in processing visual information which could help an individual to learn to read later on. In any case, a Bliss user is constantly exposed to the written word as it appears above each symbol and can be emphasised as appropriate.

Discussion Point 4:

> *'Blissymbolics has a national and international promotional network which makes it easy to obtain training and support; there is also a wide range of materials to assist in the development of educational programmes.'*

Newsletters and information sheets are circulated both nationally and internationally; displays are held, films are shown and well-prepared workshops and courses are conducted in many countries. Leading exponents of the system are enthusiastic and keen to develop new teaching strategies and to capitalise on the microelectronics revolution e.g. Cornell (1984). There are indeed many teaching materials available.

The majority of these were designed bearing in mind the needs of physically handicapped clients with receptive language already developed prior to learning the system. Resources geared to assist the language development of mentally handicapped clients are at present less extensive, but the Synrell Programmes (BCI 1985) have been devised to teach elementary sentence constructions and suggestions for teaching strategies for this group of clients can be found in the *Handbook of Blissymbolics* (Silverman *et al.*).

Peabody Rebus and Developments of Rebus

A rebus can be defined as the pictorial representation of a word. The term is derived from a plural form of the Latin word meaning 'thing' and rebuses contrast with letters which represent sounds rather than things.

The Peabody Rebus Reading Program

The 'rebus principle' was discussed in the introductory section of this chapter. As a system, however, Rebus was devised for the Peabody Rebus Reading Program, whose authors were based at the George Peabody College, Tennessee (Woodcock, Clark and Davies 1968).

At the outset there was no intention that it should be used for communication and in fact the programme was part of a wider project for teaching reading to young disadvantaged and mentally handicapped children in Chicago and Detroit. It introduces common early reading vocabulary items in a generally representational form, gradually incorporating phonic elements (i.e. letters as they sound). Within a step-by-step teaching format, which places special emphasis on comprehension skills, the transition is made to TO (i.e. Traditional Orthography or spelled words). The total programme incorporates three programmed workbooks and two readers. Conventional English sentence structures are used.

Figure 3.8: Rebus Pictographic Symbols

BIRD   CRY   BALL

Types of symbol vary. Many of the basic nouns and verbs are pictographic, as in Figure 3.8. Some are ideographic, representing an idea in relatively concrete form. Rebus often makes use of geometric shapes, as in Figure 3.9. Some of the symbols are arbitrary and abstract, as in Figure 3.10. Sometimes

Figure 3.9: Rebus Ideographic Symbols Based on Geometric Shapes

AT   BIG   SMALL

Figure 3.10: Rebus Abstract Symbols

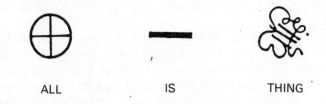

ALL   IS   THING

Figure 3.11: Rebus Symbols Based on Homonyms

BE   NOT

Figure 3.12: Rebus Symbols Incorporating Phonic Elements

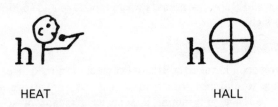

HEAT   HALL

homonyms are used, in accordance with the 'rebus principle', i.e. a word is indicated by the representation of something with a similar sound. This is illustrated in Figure 3.11, where a picture of a bee represents BE and a knot represents NOT. Letters are combined with other symbols of any type to form new words, as in Figure 3.12. Culturally conventional symbols are also included in the vocabulary, such as a plus sign for AND and an equals sign for ARE.

The total number of vocabulary items in the programme is 172. Their nature and scope resembles that of other more conventional reading schemes, rather than being geared to everyday communication. Many more rebuses are available in the *Standard Rebus Glossary* (Clark, Davies and Woodcock 1974) which enlarges the vocabulary to over 800 items – more than enough for the individual communication needs of most mentally handicapped people. Consideration of the appropriateness of the symbols for this population is given under Discussion Point 1.

MELDS

Associated with Peabody Rebus is *The Minnesota Early Language Development Sequence* or MELDS (Clark, Moores and Woodcock 1975). This is a receptive language program for hearing-impaired children with little or no language. It has also been used with severely mentally handicapped people.

Parallel tuition is given in symbols from the *Standard Rebus Glossary* (Clark *et al.* 1974), American Sign Language (ASL) and speech. Sentence patterns of spoken English are taught in the course of a structured program, which stresses the equivalence of object, symbol, sign and spoken word. A variety of instructional materials are available and also the *MELDS Glossary of Rebuses and Signs* (Clark and Greco 1973), which presents nearly 400 pairs of rebuses and signs used together in the program.

Clark Early Language Program

A more recent Rebus publication, also from the USA, is the *Clark Early Language Program* or CELP (Clark and Moores 1984). This offers grammatical instruction and practice in using several parts of speech and simple sentence constructions. In 55 developmental lessons it aims to teach functional language, both receptive and expressive, to students with language or hearing impairment. Using a Total Communication approach, the program involves about 150 Rebus symbols, spoken language and (optionally) Signed English (SE) signing.

Rebus Developments in the UK

A research project undertaken at Bristol Polytechnic aimed to teach rebuses as a first language to children with neither receptive nor expressive language (Jones 1978). Such a programme is seen as a means of accelerating the development of normal speech. The early teaching procedure, which closely resembles that used by Deich and Hodges, is described in Chapter 5. Jones (1979) notes that the children following the programme began to vocalise when they had learnt approximately 30 rebuses.

Another British development of Rebus originated at the Rees Thomas School for severely mentally handicapped children in Cambridge (van Oosterom and Devereux 1982). Judy van Oosterom adapted the published *Peabody Rebus Reading Program* for concept development and language acquisition as well as using it to introduce reading skills. She comments that some of the pupils progressed to reading traditional orthography (TO). Many of her teaching methods are described in *Learning with Rebuses* (Devereux and van Oosterom 1984).

Van Oosterom redesigned a number of the Peabody Rebus symbols, in particular replacing those which Fristoe and Lloyd (1979) describe as 'semantically aberrant', including the bee for BE and knot for NOT. A compilation of her symbols appears in *Learning with Rebuses Glossary* (van Oosterom and Devereux 1984).

Discussion Point 1:

 'Many Rebuses are unsuitable for mentally handicapped people either conceptually or for other reasons.'

The punning and 'semantically aberrant' Rebus symbols are potentially confusing to a mentally handicapped individual who is being taught to read symbols for meaning. However, many of these symbols are inessential and recently issued teaching materials have replaced the puns which occur regularly with abstract symbols. This obviates the possible confusion, though as discussed earlier arbitrary and abstract symbols are more difficult to learn than concrete ones. The conventionally well known symbols like the plus and equals signs will be unfamiliar to most mentally handicapped people prior to following one of the language programmes and so will also appear arbitrary.

A number of Rebus symbols differ only slightly from each other, which may make distinguishing between them difficult for a severely mentally handicapped person. As illustrated in Figure 3.13, FROM only differs from OFF by virtue of the added dot; UP and DOWN show the same arrow in exactly opposite orientations and ON and UNDER are little more than reorientations of each other.

Figure 3.13: Rebus Symbol Pairs with Minimal Differences

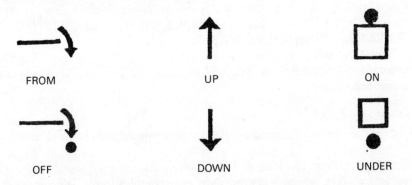

The meaning of BIG and SMALL respectively (see Figure 3.9) can only be determined by assessing the scale that is implied by the adjacent symbols. The cognitive skill required to carry out such a task is appreciably more advanced than is needed to undertstand the concepts themselves.

Peabody Rebus symbols made up of a letter of the alphabet plus a non-alphabetic symbol (cf. Figure 3.12) may be conceptually confusing. Where one part of the composite symbol is strongly iconic, as is the man eating in $h + EAT = HEAT$, the iconic part will have a greater impact than the meaning of the symbol as a whole.

Thus, while the majority of iconic Rebus symbols are quite transparent and easy for a mentally handicapped client to relate to, the initial comment regarding unsuitability can be justified when applied to the less pictorial or composite Rebuses.

Discussion Point 2:

'The Peabody Rebus Reading Program reinforces the development of language for communication.'

In presenting their rationale for the Reading Program, the authors point to the way the Rebus system is used as a link between the spoken language and reading: a basic vocabulary of Rebus symbols can be learnt in a few minutes and passages composed of these symbols read out immediately. As Buckley (1984) notes the acquisition of reading skills can improve the speech of some mentally handicapped children.

A pupil who follows the *Introducing Reading* workbooks belonging to the scheme practises answering multiple-choice questions designed to improve his cognitive skill as well as specific reading skills. Greater cognitive skill gives a firmer base for linguistic development.

However, the stories do not pertain to everyday experiences (e.g. to quote from the second reader: 'The umbrellas are good for fleas who like to ride down to the ground'). The vocabulary, which is compiled to correspond with conventional 'pre-primer' and early reading schemes, includes several words unlikely to be needed in day-to-day communication and omits a number which frequently occur (e.g. APPLE, BISCUIT/COOKIE, MORE, TOILET/BATHROOM and WASH).

Therefore, while in general terms the Reading Program may reinforce language development, its thrust is not towards language for communication purposes.

Discussion Point 3:

'The social skill of communication is not promoted in Rebus programmes.'

Although smiling, touching and wordless vocalising are part of very early communication, language is needed for more complex forms. When mentally handicapped people have failed to pick up language skills through incidental social learning, the most effective teaching often takes place one to one. This is where the stress lies in Rebus programmes from the USA, though, for example, the Rebus Word Cards are quite large enough for use in group instruction. In 'Rebus at Rees Thomas School' (van Oosterom and Devereux 1982) and *Learning with Rebuses* (Devereux and van Oosterom 1984), the authors describe games which two children can play together and note the use of the system in encouraging group participation.

Rebus symbols can provide a very suitable focus for group activities involving social interaction, which can run in parallel with other individually based programmes.

Discussion Point 4:

'The American signing component of MELDS and the Clark Early Language Program (CELP) renders them impractical for British use.'

With the MELDS program, American Sign Language (ASL) signing is incorporated and with the CELP program, American Signed English (SE). Therefore as they stand they are not very suitable for non-American clients.

The CELP program can still provide a structure for learning without the involvement of signing, since that component is optional. However, for mentally handicapped people with impaired speech and other learning difficulties, the use of signing alongside symbols and the spoken word is a valuable aid. If the signing component were to be changed to British Sign Language (BSL) or British SE, a number of symbols whose design depends on the signs would have to be redesigned to correspond (some are already available in the *Learning with Rebuses Glossary* (van Oosterom and Devereux 1984). Another strategy would be to substitute Sigsymbols, which are already designed to link up with BSL signs. With these changes, the programs become equally practical for a British clientele.

Sigsymbols

A Sigsymbol is an outline drawing depicting a single concept. Each is enclosed within a square box or on an individual card. The drawings are executed in black with red insertions to emphasise certain aspects of significance; in an alternative version for photocopying, the red lines are replaced by black lines of a contrasting thickness to the rest, consistently either finer or bolder. (Bold lines, like the red, stand out well, but fine lines can be more satisfactorily traced over in red after photocopying.) Sigsymbols may be of any size, depending on the nature of the educational experience.

Of the symbols systems described in this book, Sigsymbols is the only one that was designed from the outset for use by mentally handicapped people. One of the present authors, Ailsa Cregan, devised them as a teaching tool for the development of language and communication while she was working with a group of institutionalised young teenagers, all of whom were severely mentally handicapped. Two members of the group were occasionally withdrawn for tuition in signing (Makaton) which, however, had failed to generalise to spontaneous use. This was the initial spur for the invention of Sigsymbols. It also led to the decision to link them with signs and call them *Sig*symbols, a contraction of sign-symbols.

In devising the system, Bloom and Lahey's (1978) model of language was borne in mind, with its three essential interdependent areas: content, involving meaningful concepts and message; use, involving social interaction and appropriateness of context; and form, involving word combinations and structured language. The problems to be combated included difficulties in attention, visual discrimination, short-term memory and the combining and sequencing of words, as an outcome of the children's limited cognitive ability. Their expressive language was severely impaired or lacking, though all had some receptive language.

The underlying theory and the practical problems indicated six criteria for an appropriate symbol system:

Decodability.   Symbols should, as far as possible, be directly meaningful and decodable in a single step.
Avoidance of Abstraction.   Symbols should relate to something concrete in the children's experience.
Clarity.   Visually the symbols should be easily discriminated. The need for fine distinctions of size, position or orientation should be avoided.
Logicality.   The system should be devised according to logical rules, a knowledge of which should facilitate deduction of symbol meaning.
Useful Vocabulary.   This was needed both for the educational setting and for social communication. According to need, it should be possible to generate additional symbols.
Reproducibility.   This should be possible quickly and easily, for spontaneous use and to allow maximum flexibility to a teacher.

A set of Sigsymbols, designed with the intention of meeting these criteria, was first published in the UK in 1982 (Cregan 1982) and consisted of 240 items.

Where a directly-meaning-based symbol is practicable, Sigsymbols are pictographic or ideographic. (Direct meaningfulness of symbols helps to promote awareness of content, and also relates to the decodability criterion.) Examples of pictographs, some with ideographic elements, are shown in Figure 3.14 and include a simplified representation (BIRD), a figure in which the posture implies movement (RUN), a face with a red/bold arrow suggesting sound going into the ear (HEAR) and the Sig for GIVE in which the red/bold arrows suggest movement of the thing that is being given. In this and other Sigs, the 'blob' is used to stand for an unspecified 'thing' when *something* is required by the meaning of the word, but should not limit the context by being specific (cf. the criterion for avoidance of the abstract).

Figure 3.14: Sigsymbol Pictographs

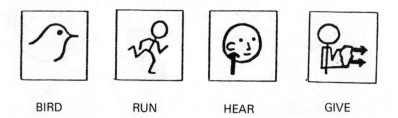

BIRD   RUN   HEAR   GIVE

Examples of ideographic Sigs are shown in Figure 3.15: SOME is represented by 'some' (unspecified) 'things', i.e. blobs; LONG is an example of the way opposites are encoded in Sig, with the significant aspect being drawn in red/bold lines, while its opposite appears beside it in black/standard lines to provide the comparison; ON and OVER belong to the set of positional prepositions which, in relation to a triangle, use a red/bold blob or arrow to illustrate a static or dynamic concept respectively. A triangle is used because it has a natural apex and base so that Sigsymbols for, e.g., ON and UNDER are distinct from each other, even when seen upside-down, as in group sessions round a table (cf. the criterion for clarity).

Figure 3.15: Sigsymbol Ideographs

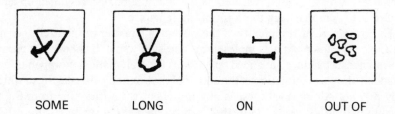

SOME   LONG   ON   OUT OF

The most distinctive feature of the Sigsymbol system is its technique for maintaining a link with the learner's concrete experience even when an abstract concept is represented. This is achieved through a series of design rules by which many Sigs are visually linked with signs – signs and Sigs being taught alongside each other to establish and reinforce the link. The rules allow additional Sigs to be generated to correspond with any sign. (Points in this paragraph relate to the criteria for avoidance of the abstract, logicality and useful vocabulary.)

The basic design rules for sign-linked Sigs are illustrated in Figure 3.16. THINK shows a schematic drawing of the right index finger pointing to the side of the head, drawn from the point of view of the signer as always in sign-linked Sigs, so as to offer support to expressive signing. QUICK shows the right index finger twice tapping the left, the movement being traced by the red/bold line. BEGIN illustrates the 'thumbs up' right hand dropping from

Figure 3.16: Sigsymbols Based on Sign Linkage

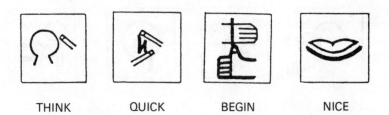

THINK   QUICK   BEGIN   NICE

above to below the flat left hand. The movement is traced by the red/bold vertical line and the right hand is also drawn in red/boldly to indicate that it has reached its final position in the sign. NICE illustrates a line being traced under the lips. The thumb which traces the line is not shown. Such omissions help to avoid visual clutter in Sigsymbols, which are designed to act as a kind of shorthand to jog the memory rather than as a complete sign representation. On a similarly practical basis, it is considered that distinctiveness of individual symbols is a higher priority than absolute consistency in translating signs into two-dimensional symbols.

As a communication system, Sigsymbols can either be presented as individual manipulable units on cards, blocks, etc. for use like symbol-shapes or can be drawn out on a communication board to be indicated by the user. If sentences or phrases are presented as a whole, the boxes are joined up as in Figure 3.17, emphasising the form of the language.

The grammatical complexity of the system is a matter of the user's (or his instructor's) choice. At its simplest, key words only should appear in a phrase or sentence. At a more advanced level, signs for grammatical morphemes can be added, drawn in miniature at the corner of the box enclosing the Sig to which they pertain. Alternatively, especially if a client is transitioning from Sig to Traditional Orthography (TO), they can be spelled out, as in Figure 3.17.

Figure 3.17: Sigsymbol Sentence Incorporating Spelled Grammatical Morphemes

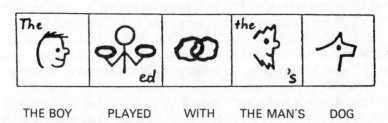

THE BOY   PLAYED   WITH   THE MAN'S   DOG

Sigsymbols were originally devised for classroom use, bearing in mind the opportunities for group tuition, which can help to promote appropriate use of the language. The game-orientated activities that are suggested by the author in the teaching pack (Cregan 1982) are a special characteristic of the system. With Sigs as a focus, matching, sorting and other activities can take place, and the signing component adds physical action to the exercise of cognitive skill and social interaction. Sig phrases and sentences can be built up in sequencing games or simple stories. The stories, whatever their level of complexity (as appropriate to the client), can then be read 'aloud' by signing or speech.

In any activity, a teacher can respond to teaching possibilities as they arise by quickly drawing new symbols (cf. the criterion for reproducibility). Cregan has found that this process in itself can be an attractive and motivating focus for those learning to use Sigsymbols.

Discussion Point 1:

'Of the symbol systems discussed, only Sig invariably encloses symbols in boxes, so the boxes are probably pointless.'

Only Sig was devised specifically for mentally handicapped people with their special needs. Many clients are distractible or pay only limited attention. Research into perception and understanding in young children (Bryant 1974) suggests that boxes help a 'reader' to perceive more clearly what is enclosed because a box and its contents are isolated and stand out clearly from their background.

The entity of the box allows another aid to perception, i.e. the Sig coding strategy for opposites, as illustrated in Figure 3.15. Within the one box it is possible to contrast the significant aspect of the symbol drawn in red/bold lines with its opposite drawn in black/standard lines. This means that dimensions are seen as relative rather than absolute, which provides a perceptual security of scale.

Singly, a box highlights the identity of an individual Sig. When boxes are joined up together, they visually reinforce the conceptual unity of a phrase or sentence.

In a number of ways, therefore, Sigsymbol boxes help to meet the needs of mentally handicapped clients.

Discussion Point 2:

'Sigsymbols have developed from a rather restricted foundation of knowledge.'

The implication of the comment is that other systems are more widely researched. Peabody Rebus, for example, was developed as part of a relatively large-scale reading research project and offshoots of that research have followed. An impressive Formative Evaluation Study of Blissymbolics gathered much information on the use of the system and many practitioners have contributed to the present body of knowledge. Some non-speech systems used by mentally handicapped people have been less substantially researched, but because of the present limited currency of Sigsymbols, even anecdotal review is not yet available from a wide range of users. Naturally this should be considered by anyone thinking of adopting the system.

On the other hand, Sigsymbols were tested in the classroom by the author and colleagues for over four years before being published, and *ad hoc* modifications were incorporated or not according to their practicality. The many Sig-based activities described in the teaching pack (some also in Chapter 5) received a similar trial by ordeal.

Professionals are urged by the author to experiment with the system, for it can co-exist with other non-speech systems within an establishment, especially with a linked signing system. At this early stage, only by experimentation with new ideas and theories will further information be forthcoming.

Discussion Point 3:

'Sigsymbols would be more logically coherent and practically useful if they set out to stimulate only one mode of communication.'

The present set of Sigsymbols is essentially a hybrid form of representation as they rely on the pictograph/ideograph as well as the sign association. Some professionals may feel that if the elicitation of signing is the aim of the system then all the symbols should correspond with signs.

By reference to the design rules, it is possible to re-design non-sign-linked Sigs to correspond with known signs; this might suit, say, a young deaf population. However, initially at least, iconic symbols are likely to be understood more easily as they are more directly meaningful. This may help to stimulate meaningful expression in whatever form. The system is flexible enough to meet a range of needs in a mixed group of speakers, signers and symbol-communicators, who might be enabled to communicate with each other. The hybrid nature of Sigsymbols may be very appropriate for the hybrid needs of mentally handicapped people.

Discussion Point 4:

'The Sigsymbol system has no organisational framework for offering training or disseminating teaching materials.'

It is true that there is no organisational framework which offers training in the use of Sigsymbols. However, the published pack, readily available from the author, contains full details of the system and suggests teaching methods and materials. It is hoped that professionals will extend and adapt these to suit their own clients.

A set of Sigs could be substituted in many programmes devised originally for other systems, and training for these may also give insights into possible ways of using Sig. The system does not set out to provide a prescriptive programme.

Instead the emphasis is on flexibility as a teaching tool for a variety of clients and settings.

Worldsign

Worldsign is a language system based on movement – a kinetic language. It can be expressed in a variety of ways: manually signed, handwritten, printed, and reproduced in animated versions for computer graphics, film and video. When animated, each symbol is said to have its own 'kinetic signature'.

The development of the system is still continuing. It was invented by David Orcutt, a puppeteer and multi-media communicator, whose knowledge of world cultural differences is reflected in his 'kinegraphs' (i.e. 'movement-writings'). He sees Worldsign as a link between people of different nations and languages, based on a kind of 'think-feeling' which stimulates interaction between the transmitter and receiver, even when the symbols are read in static graphic form.

Although Bliss's and Orcutt's ideals of world intercommunication are similar, their systems are very different. While Blissymbols are drawn with scientific precision, Orcutt's 'icons' (images) are dynamic, aiming to reflect the sign-movements of American Sign Language (ASL) in screen graphics or freely drawn symbols, often representing diagrammatic hands or other human features as in action while communicating (see Figure 3.18).

Figure 3.18: Worldsign Symbols Showing Parts of the Body and Reflecting American Sign Language Signs

PEACEFUL   AGAIN   PAIN

A core vocabulary is made up of around 600 items which can be combined in various ways to form thousands of compound meanings. Unlike Bliss 'combines', Worldsign compounds are not necessarily arranged in linear fashion. One example is given in Figure 3.19, as drawn by Orcutt himself (Orcutt 1983). This example also illustrates the very flexible grammar of Worldsign: parts of speech, depending on need and context, can change from one category to another and word order can be freely varied.

Worldsign was only made public in the early 1980s, and although one or two articles on it have appeared in the USA (e.g. Warrick 1984), the authors have

Figure 3.19: Worldsign Sentence Showing Flexible Grammar and Presentation

WORLDSIGN HELPS EMERGE FROM SOURCE
WHOLE WORLD INTERCONNECTED FEEL-THINKING

found no reference to it in British educational literature. It is therefore hardly surprising that specific applications for handicapped people have not yet been outlined, though Orcutt (1984) suggests that, because of its multi-sensory approach, it may have particular advantages for this section of the community. This belief is based on psycho-neurological theory and his own knowledge of Japanese writing. In Japanese writing there is a syllabic component with symbols based on sound as well as an ideographic component with symbols based on meaning. Reportedly, some Japanese people with brain damage lose only the ability to write in the syllabic component, while retaining ideographic ability. This may imply that iconic (representational) and phonic (sound-based) writing are processed in different areas of the brain. Because Worldsign functions visually and through movement, Orcutt believes it may be processed in the right-hand brain hemisphere, bypassing any damage in the left-hand brain hemisphere which normally processes linguistic abstractions. Thus it has the potential to assist many people with learning difficulties.

Discussion Point 1:

> *'Since several symbol systems already exist for non-speech communication, another one is not needed.'*

If the new system closely resembled existing ones, this statement would undoubtedly be true. However, Worldsign is very original in its multi-modal, multi-sensory approach and its use of microtechnology as an integral part of the system, whereas other systems have come to exploit its capacities at a later stage in their development.

Worldsign has not yet had time to prove itself, either with handicapped or non-handicapped users; it is still developing and has already been modified considerably in use. Its originality makes the system of interest, and novelty alone is insufficient reason for rejecting it.

Discussion Point 2:

> '*Available written examples of Worldsign would be confusing for mentally handicapped people, difficult for them to decipher and impracticable for them to draw.*'

Many symbols do share a family resemblance, which could be confusing (see Figure 3.20). This can make discrimination difficult and it is not eased by the small size and rather cramped layout of many of the available written examples (Orcutt 1983). However, there are no rules restricting modification of the symbols to make them clearer for a mentally handicapped user, for example by tracing salient aspects of symbols in a different colour. Size and layout are a matter of taste, convenience and appropriateness to the context.

Figure 3.20: Worldsign Symbol Pairs with Minimal Differences

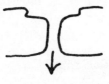

WITH

CAN

NEED

YOU

In computer graphics, distinctive movement of the symbols makes them easier to identify. The animation may also encourage a client to look more attentively at the symbols, perhaps later transferring his attention and understanding to the static form of the symbols.

The impracticability of clients drawing the symbols for themselves applies to most symbol systems, not only Worldsign. For expressive use they might appear on a communication board or as individual symbol units or provide support for American Sign Language (ASL) signing. Alternatively, a computer interface would make possible mechanical selection of an animated display of symbols.

Discussion Point 3:

> *'The flexibility of Worldsign makes it appropriate for a wide range of client needs.'*

The rationale of Worldsign means it can provide a choice of expressive options (see previous discussion point) to any of which clients may respond.

However, its use of a 'combine' strategy may hinder decodability and distance it from spoken English. As its signing component is ASL, the system would need extensive modification for use outside a North American context. Its freedom from rules of design or syntax may easily result in unsystematic visual or grammatical presentation, whereas there is general agreement on the need to be systematic with mentally handicapped clients. The philosophy of feel-thinking is not readily encompassed within a structured behavioural programme.

Nevertheless, although various characteristics of Worldsign restrict its appropriateness for many mentally handicapped clients, it has been included among the systems discussed because it offers a thought-provoking and contemporary approach.

Alphabetic Script

When the form of symbols relates to their meaning, as in representational pictographs, they are quite easy to understand. However, a potentially enormous number of symbols is needed for a 1:1 ratio of symbols to words or concepts. Reducing the number of symbols that are needed by the strategy of combining them to signify new meanings makes for more efficient 'writing' but a less direct relationship between symbol and meaning. There are fewer symbols to learn and remember, but analytical decoding requires more than one step.

The alphabet with its very small number of symbols is a highly efficient writing medium, but does have disadvantages. Firstly, individual letters are relatively similar and difficult to discriminate, and secondly, words have absolutely no visual relationship with their meaning. Furthermore, the process of analytically decoding spelled words is complex: each (abstract) letter must be (arbitrarily) linked with a sound and then the blended sounds that make up the whole must be (arbitrarily) linked with the meaning.

The look-and-say approach provides a rather more direct route, for a whole word is recognised and named (i.e. read) as a unit. This early reading method is generally preferred for mentally handicapped children and older clients – though a danger to be avoided is 'barking at print', i.e. reading aloud, perhaps quite fluently, but without comprehension.

Despite the fact that some mentally handicapped people can and do learn to read, the idea of the printed word being used as an alternative means of communication or as a source for language development has only fairly recently been considered. In the UK at least there are historical reasons for this, related to the beginning of special education for severely mentally handicapped children when responsibility for it was transferred from the Department of Health to that of Education. As noted in the introduction to this book, when the transfer took place in 1971, many of the personnel entering this area of special education were experienced nursery or infant teachers or shared a similar philosophy. This not only placed a high value on discovery learning and unstructured verbal enrichment, but held that the teaching of the three Rs had been over-emphasised. It was generally considered that special education settings were not appropriate for promoting such an academic tradition – a view that was particularly understandable since the current teaching methods were not producing encouraging results.

The introduction of structured behavioural methods gave more grounds for optimism since 'academic' attainments like a reading vocabulary could be systematically taught, step by step. Specific goals for language development could be reached in the same way.

Recent projects and publications have encouraged an active approach to teaching mentally handicapped children to read, seeing reading as a 'way in' to language development and a stimulus to the use of speech.

Sue Buckley, Senior Psychologist at Portsmouth Polytechnic, has researched into the teaching of young Down's Syndrome children. Though her original programme was aimed at relatively intelligent handicapped children, it is an approach worth considering for a wider range of clients. The programme (briefly and clearly described in *Reading and Language Development in Children with Down's Syndrome* (Buckley 1984)) uses pictures to help the child understand and use a first vocabulary of about 50 words. At this point he is expected to move on to flashcards with printed words – matching them, then selecting one as requested, then naming them. When the child begins to read himself, the material is geared to his level of language development; for example, if he uses phrases of two words only, he is given two-word phrases to read. The importance of parents reading to their children and conversing with them in 'real-life' situations is strongly emphasised, with the aim of extending vocabulary and reinforcing understanding.

Other approaches which have worked well with handicapped children are described in *Teaching Reading to Mentally Handicapped Children* (Thatcher 1984), including one which uses pictures as a bridge to the words in short sentences. Thatcher describes his imaginative teaching methods in detail.

Another technique is that of the Peabody Rebus Reading Program (Woodcock *et al.* 1969). Using non-alphabetic Rebus symbols, the child is familiarised with the reading process. Spelled words are introduced one by one, initially overprinted in yellow to highlight their newness, with the symbol printed above them. When the two have become associated in the reader's mind, first the symbol is omitted and then the yellow overprinting. Reading some Rebus vocabulary depends on an analysis of the way the words sound, which, as discussed earlier, is not usually the most practical strategy for severely mentally handicapped people, but the programme does provide a structured teaching framework.

A quite different approach to the acquisition of a reading vocabulary is to change the nature of print so that it possesses some pictorial qualities. 'Symbol accentuation' was pioneered in the USA (Miller 1968), designed for use with severely mentally handicapped people. In the UK, its promotion has mainly been through a book, *Let Me Read* (Jeffree and Skeffington 1980). Symbol accentuation attempts to bridge the gap between picture and abstract symbol recognition by changing the shape of a word so that its form is intermediate between the word itself and the representation of its meaning (see Figure 3.21). With imagination, ingenious and distinctive accentuated symbols can be produced.

Figure 3.21: Symbol Accentuation Showing its Intermediate Position between Word and Picture

CUP

One of the present authors, Philip Jones (Jones 1983), has completed a limited but controlled study which indicated that words were more easily taught by accentuating them than by placing them, unaccentuated, below a key picture. However, a disadvantage of the method is the difficulty of accentuating many of the words in common written or spoken use, even excluding those which are relatively abstract.

Another option is simply to elaborate already-printed material with pencil additions. In comparing the effectiveness of this approach to conventional symbol accentuation, Jones found it was equally effective in teaching a sight vocabulary to a mentally handicapped child. He suggests that elaboration is an easier way of giving words a more concrete form. Two examples are illustrated in Figure 3.22. A precise structure for teaching vocabulary with the help of elaboration has yet to be devised and evaluated.

Most approaches to communication using the written word are variants of the look-and-say reading method which, without reference to the sound-values

Figure 3.22: Two Methods of Pictorialising Spelled Words:
          A. Symbol Accentuation
          B. Word Elaboration

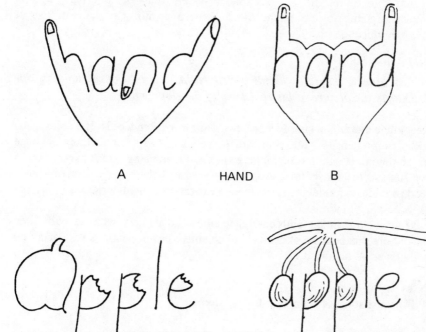

    A   HAND   B

    A   APPLE   B

of letters, can provide an extensive vocabulary. (Buckley (1984) mentions one child who learnt a sight vocabulary of 600 words.) Written or printed, words can appear on communication boards, individual cards or card-strips, and their expressive use can be similar to that of non-alphabetic symbols – provided, of course, that a client finds them equally meaningful. Like these, they can also offer a permanently visible cue for expression by means of signing or speech and their grammatical complexity can be tailored to individual needs.

Discussion Point 1:

  'Using alphabetic script is a very desirable method of non-speech communication as it is quite acceptable to the wider community.'

The obvious advantage of conventional script over other systems is that it minimises the differences between the handicapped person and the rest of society. Nor do families have to set about learning a new system. Furthermore, to parents and others, 'literacy' appears as a solid achievement. Word recognition is a conventional element of ever child's schooling, which can be cited as evidence of progress.

However, in the present context, the aim is to provide a *communication* system. No matter how acceptable a system may be to others, if it is not meaningful to the client himself there is no way he can use it to communicate.

Discussion Point 2:

  'Teaching a mentally handicapped child to read conventional script distorts the picture of his real level of development.'

Reading is more than simply a rote response to written words. If a child reads with comprehension, the skill can serve as a basis for further language development. It can, for example, give practice in using words in context, so contributing to concept formation and extension. The linguistic form of what is read provides a model for spontaneous expression, giving practice in the use of word combinations.

When a child understands enough to enjoy and act upon what he reads, then the picture that is given of his level of cognitive development is very accurate and not at all distorted.

A Comparison between Symbol Systems

As with signs, we need to think in terms of the target population and the needs of its members when making comparisons between symbol systems. Five different aspects will be discussed. Little attention will be given in this section to pictures and to the alphabet: pictures because they hardly constitute a 'system' and the alphabet because it is qualitatively different from the other systems described, which may have little in common but are all basically non-alphabetic.

Decodability of Symbols

A symbol system which is easily decoded is more meaningful to the user. Two features affecting decodability are whether the symbols are iconic and whether decoding can be achieved in a single step.

Clark's (1981) study comparing the learning of traditional orthography (TO) and three symbol systems found that the most iconic system, Rebus, was significantly easier to learn than Bliss, which is also iconic but less manifestly so. (In fact, many of the iconic Blissymbols are so simplified that mentally handicapped clients may not recognise their representational nature.) However, both Rebus and Bliss were significantly easier to learn than the arbitrarily shaped Non-SLIP symbols.

Of the systems not covered by the study, Sigsymbols and Worldsign also contain some obviously pictorial symbols and when symbolising abstract concepts both avoid abstract symbols by employing sign linkage. The decodability of such symbols depends on whether they really do evoke the signs.

Non-SLIP and many Deich and Hodges symbols, in which even concrete concepts are represented by abstract shapes, do have the advantage of being decodable in one step, unlike composite Rebus symbols and Bliss combines. Of course the meaningfulness of the shapes depends on the clients' recall of the concepts arbitrarily attached to the non-iconic shapes.

Logicality/Deducibility/Generation of New Vocabulary

The advantage of logical design rules in a system is that they facilitate the deduction of non-iconic symbol meanings. They also permit the generation of new symbols which can be recognised as belonging to the system.

As Non-SLIP and most Deich and Hodges symbol-shapes are arbitrary, their meaning cannot be deduced. Generating more arbitrarily shaped symbols would not be too difficult, but memorising the meaning of large numbers of them would be much less easy.

Two systems have principles laid down for the generation of new symbols. There are general principles for designing pictographic and ideographic Sigsymbols and specific rules for sign-linked symbols. For this, of course, a knowledge of signs is necessary; someone already possessing a knowledge of signs might deduce the meaning of corresponding Sigsymbols. The Blissymbol 'combine' strategy is a very creative and logical way of generating new vocabulary; however, while the meaning should be deducible by an able person, for a mentally handicapped person analysis of the 'combines' to decode them may present problems.

Ceiling of Expression/Relation to Structure of Spoken English

The expressive potential of different systems varies. Many clients will not need a wide range of expression and their single-word or telegraphic messages may make grammatical considerations irrelevant. On the other hand, more able clients, especially those who may develop speech, may be better served by a system which can support the grammatical construction of more complex messages.

Expression with Deich and Hodges symbol shapes is restricted to the concrete. Symbol order contributes to meaning, but grammar is not involved as such. Non-SLIP vocabulary and grammatical construction is intentionally limited and inflexible, not well suited to communicative use. Sigsymbols can support simple or less simple expression according to need; English word order is recommended, key words only, or a fuller reflection of speech, with or without grammatical morphemes. The range of Rebus is similar.

The most flexible, subtle and wide-ranging expression is offered by Bliss, which can meet the needs of intellectually normal people. Grammatical construction can reflect speech, but experienced users suggest that the system has developed a grammar of its own which departs from spoken constructions though is visually more expressive.

Ease of Discrimination

The need for fine discrimination can be a disadvantage if – as is often the case with mentally handicapped people – clients' attention is intermittent or superficial or they suffer from perceptual problems.

Leaving aside the alphabet, the system which is most demanding is Bliss, since symbol size and position must be finely differentiated to determine meaning (cf. Figure 3.7 above), and as many symbols are straight reversals of each other orientation is also important. Within the Rebus system, size and orientation of symbols can also be significant, though for a relatively small number of symbols. Position is not critical.

The remaining systems make comparatively few demands on fine discrimination. Sigsymbols specifically avoids reversals and the size and position of symbols is not significant. Within-symbol points of reference are provided to assist discrimination (cf. LONG and ON in Figure 3.15 and the accompanying discussion). Worldsign symbols are intended to be freely drawn, depending on context and intention of users. Symbol shapes in Non-SLIP and the Deich and Hodges system do have a conventional orientation, but reorientation does not affect meaning, nor does the size and relative position of symbols.

Reproducibility

Symbols appearing on a communication board need not be readily reproducible as they can be pointed at repeatedly. Nor do individual symbol units need reproduction when a given vocabulary is being used regularly to convey simple messages. However, within a teaching situation, reproducibility is important to facilitate a quick response when new teaching opportunities arise.

Made out of plastic, as the originals were, symbol-shapes are not very easy to reproduce, though it would be possible – if rather slow – to trace, cut out and colour cardboard approximations. Blissymbols in themselves are simple to draw, though the need for precision imposes constraints and freehand drawing is not recommended by Bliss instructors. Templates are available to make precision possible, but only in a limited number of sizes; when other sizes are required, the basic grid should be roughed to provide a guideline.

In contrast, Sigsymbols were designed for freehand drawing, requiring two contrasting pens but no particular artistic skill. From Rebus and Worldsign, many symbols would be easy to draw, though there are also a number of quite elaborate pictographs not so easily copied.

Figure 3.23 summarises the points of comparison that have been discussed, but is not intended to suggest that there is a 'best buy' among symbol systems.

Figure 3.23: Characteristics of Six Symbol Systems

	Non-SLIP	Deich and Hodges	Rebus	Bliss	Worldsign	Sigsymbols
Iconic/transparent	–		+		+	+
Avoidance of abstract and arbitrary	–	–			+	+
Available/logically extendable vocabulary	–	· –	Assoc. progs +	+	+	+
Ceiling of expression	–	–		+		
Possible reflection of grammar of speech	(+)	–	+	+		+
Lower discrimination requirements	+	+		–		+
Easy reproducibility			Some	+	+	+

On its own, a table of comparisons gives too simplistic a view on which to base a choice of system for a particular client and setting, but does provide information for quick reference.

4 COMMUNICATION AIDS AND ACCESSING

This chapter looks at means by which mentally handicapped clients with additional handicaps can be helped to use a non-speech system.

After a brief consideration of the physical management of multiply handicapped clients, the special needs of those with visual impairment are touched upon. We then discuss factors influencing the choice of a communication aid. Next, various strategies for selecting the components of a message are outlined, followed by a description of different types of switching device by which clients can gain access to electronic equipment. (Unavoidably, since the nature of a symbol display, the selection strategy and the equipment may be interdependent, descriptions of them sometimes overlap.) Finally, aids for stimulating very passive or low-functioning clients are considered; these may arouse them to greater awareness and so help to motivate communication.

Seating, Signing and Visual Handicap

Technical intervention in manual signing amounts to very little, except in terms of seating, standing frames and accessories which assist the positioning and stability of a physically handicapped person. However, these may be vital if he is to sign clearly and comfortably and are also relevant when symbols in a display must be pointed at. When an individual language programme is being planned, a physiotherapist or occupational therapist may be able to advise on appliances relating to physical management. Despite the importance of such appliances, their function is not directly communicative, so details will not be given here. Readers seeking further information may wish to consult *Treatment of Cerebral Palsy and Motor Delay* (Levitt 1979), especially Chapter 6 on sitting development, and the section entitled 'Positioning and Handtraining Towards Symbol Usage' in the *Handbook of Blissymbolics* (Silverman *et al.* 1978).

Use of a signing system will be restricted if a client's poor sight allows him to distinguish only gross movements, for he will be unable to 'read' other people's signs. However, if he cannot speak but has learnt how to make signs with the help of touch and feel, other people will be able to 'read' what he signs. Their communication in return may be through speech.

If a visually impaired client is to be provided with symbols, some accommodation can be made for his disability. Large-size, extra-boldly-drawn symbols may help, or they can be cut out of sandpaper and stuck on a rigid backing so discrimination can be assisted by touch. The categories of individual symbols can also be defined by tactile cues: different sets can be distinguished by blocks of different thicknesses, or the surface of some cards can be roughened by sticking on a sprinkle of sand or made shiny by a covering of clear sticky-backed plastic. Alternatively, different bright colours of card can define different sets.

Choosing an Aid

Electronic communication aids are less easily constructed on a do-it-yourself basis. Moreover, owing to the rapid advances of the micro-electronics revolution, items which are a novelty one year may be obsolescent the next. Not only are they quickly superseded, but the typically small scale of production may preclude commercial availability. Thus there is little point in aiming to detail the latest innovation; our intention is rather to outline general principles so that the reader is in a position to make sense of the products flowing on and off the market.

Choosing the right aid is a highly individual matter. Nevertheless, client, carer and any professional involved may have to make do with provision which is determined by outside factors or by people other than themselves. Finance plays a part if the aid is publicly funded: for example, prior to the 1981 Education Act if not thereafter, UK education budgets were allocated with more regard to group and institutional utility than to individual needs. (Paradoxically, the reverse is the case with equipment supplied by the Department of Health and Social Security.) Unfortunately, at times the determining factors appear to have been idiosyncratic or inflexible ideas about the needs of handicapped people. If money is to be spent wisely on the most appropriate equipment, then the arbiters of these matters require regularly updated knowledge and understanding of specialist work being done in the field.

Apart from the obvious consideration of purchase price, practicalities should influence the choice of any aid to communication. Robustness and reliability are a priority since a user is greatly inconvenienced when his aid is out of action and the cost of even minor repairs to a piece of high-tech equipment can be prohibitive unless undertaken by an expert friend, volunteer or member of the family. Portability makes an aid more convenient, and in the life-style of some clients it may be essential. Another factor to consider is the possibility of direct selection of symbols, especially if the client's level of cognitive functioning is doubtful. A facility for at least semi-permanently recording the symbols that have been selected may also be desirable.

In the past, the above characteristics were often lacking from more electronically sophisticated pieces of equipment, so that on occasions a user really needed a more portable, low-tech aid instead. Nowadays, however, many very internally complex aids are quite reliable and portable. Direct selection of symbols is frequently possible and devices are user-friendly.

When the larger, not-so-portable items which are difficult to use in a flexible, social manner are superseded as everyday communication aids, they may still have a useful function as pieces of teaching equipment.

Selection Strategies

Thanks to the range of technical innovation, it is possible for a person to indicate his choice of vocabulary items in a variety of different ways. Essentially, however, these techniques are variations or combinations of the elementary strategies of scanning, encoding or direct selection. In this section, the merits and disadvantages of each of these approaches are considered.

Scanning

When an individual is presented with a sequenced list of items seen or heard, he must scan them to find the one he requires. The strategy often develops naturally between a non-speaking person and others; usually in this case the presentation is verbal and the items are restricted to a small number which are relevant to the context of the conversation.

Even if no firm concept of 'yes' and 'no' has been established, or an individual has found no way of indicating alternatives, he may be able simply to affirm the presence of the 'correct' item. The smallest physical response suffices for such limited communication, such as a nod of the head or some kind of vocalisation. Only very rarely is special technology required to facilitate this kind of communication.

Not all handicapped people can understand spoken words. For them the presentation of pictures, symbols, objects or even events may be more meaningful. In the last instance, if the choice was between, say, going to the lavatory and food, the individual's different responses when taken to the bathroom and dining area could be observed. This rather cumbersome procedure elicits a primitive scanning technique. (If large-size symbols signifying the areas are clearly visible in the areas themselves, and the client's attention drawn to them on every visit, it may eventually become possible to fade in the use of symbols to replace actual visits.)

Although such an interpersonal style of presentation has the advantages of spontaneity, economy of given choices and direct social contact, it does not allow for much independence. Some multiply handicapped people whose expressive whims are sought perhaps too patiently by staff, friends or family may become passively self-centred. Very direct methods such as the above allow no visible recording of the language used and only very simple communication is supported.

Scanning as described may appear to be a lengthy process. However, the options can be varied infinitely and no technical display can emulate such an intelligent use of context. Mechanical or electronic systems may be quicker in presenting different items, but the number of items has to be far greater to ensure that the appropriate one is available. In addition, the client's attention has to be more concentrated or he may miss the desired item and, unless his affirmative response is obvious, his 'conversant' must be very ready to observe it (the term 'conversant' is used here and subsequently as a concise way of referring to whoever is trying to converse with the mentally handicapped person).

One adaptation of the scanning technique is for the options to be displayed *en bloc*, rather than being presented in sequence. Pointing is then used to indicate the chosen item. Such a display differs from a verbal presentation in that the vocabulary range is more restricted, but it does mean that the options can all be under consideration at once and the handicapped person can review them in his own good time. With the help of technology, visual displays can be scanned by mechanical or electronic means, sometimes by a flashing light passing back and forth along the lines of symbols displayed on a communication board or by a rotating arrow pointing to items in a circular array of symbols (see Figure 4.1).

Figure 4.1: Devices for Linear and Circular Scanning of Symbols

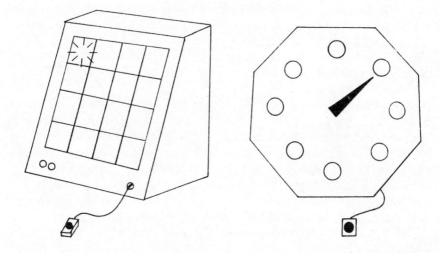

On older equipment, scanning usually proceeded continuously and cyclically until an affirmative response was made. Some more modern devices can keep an option open until a client is ready to progress to the next item. Of course with this method two responses are required, one for progression to the next item and one to affirm the currently indicated item. It is much slower than automatic progression and requires a more continuous active response from the client. On the other hand, it does mean that he is in charge of the scanning operation and able to work at his own speed, which makes for more accurate selection. The flexibility allows him to be less careful when the display is being scanned well away from the target and then to slow down the pointer to make sure the item he wants to select is not missed.

All the above scanning techniques rely on the 'conversant' keeping track of the communication and if necessary reminding the client of his message. While this is quite acceptable in conversation, for specific language tuition it is preferable to have a semi-permanent visual record of the immediately preceding conversation, especially when 'utterances' extend to more than one or two words. Sometimes the lights of an electronic aid can be left on till the end of an 'utterance', but this has the disadvantage that when several static items on a display board are illuminated together, no sequencing is apparent. As a result, the feedback from the display gives no reinforcement to the expression and understanding of correctly sequenced language (see Figure 4.2).

Figure 4.2: Illuminated Display Board with Memory

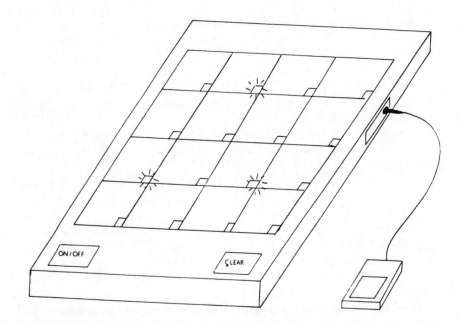

Some devices do in fact permit the 'utterance' to be displayed in sequential form, independent of the layout of the full array of symbols. The display can be maintained either printed out on a paper strip or on a VDU (i.e. electronic visual display unit or screen). Although these linear memories have the advantage of encouraging structured language, they provide only an indirect link between the handicapped person's expression and its display. For some clients, the necessary transfer of attention may be too cognitively demanding to be meaningful.

In recent years, voice-encoding devices have become available, with a cross-modal memory that allows a client to select a symbol by visual scanning, following which the device 'speaks' the equivalent word.

Direct Selection

When employing direct selection, a person indicates the elements of his message by immediate contact. The use of gesture is less sophisticated than verbal scanning, but is one method of direct selection often generated spontaneously by someone without speech. It may then be followed by some other form of scanning if a vocabulary item is not within view or if finer interpretation is needed after the initial broad gesture.

Direct selection of symbols on a display board requires some physical ability. Finger-pointing is the most commonly used technique and — given the physical capability — the simplest. However, the degree of physical handicap may militate against clear selection; for example, involuntary writhing movements as in athetoid cerebral palsy, or unsteady muscular control from whatever cause, make it difficult to pinpoint one item in a display. The client's indication may not be precise enough for the 'conversant' to determine what has been selected. The wrong finger or a different part of the hand may be interpreted as making the selection. Clarity is even more problematic as the range of vocabulary extends and the symbols on a manageably sized communication board get smaller.

These difficulties can be ameliorated to some extent by pointing aids or by modifications to equipment. Symbols which are guarded or indented can make the confusion of items less likely and provide a purchase point to help stabilise the selection. A board may be surfaced with non-slip material. A client who has a reasonably firm grasp may be helped by a grippable magnetic arrow to place on a board with a suitable surface. More complicated mechanical or electronic means of pointing may be employed: a light pointer, for example, beams a bright spot which can be directed at symbols on a carefully placed communication board. A client with good head control might have a light pointer or stick pointer attached to his head — or indeed to any part of his body which he was able to control.

Some clients are able to develop skill in eye-pointing. For this, the method of presentation is crucial. Though it may be possible to display a succession of vocabulary sheets, the number of items on display at any one time is necessarily very limited. Unless the symbols are large or widely separated, it is difficult for a 'conversant' to interpret the eye-pointing precisely; the 'conversant' will in any case need to be positioned directly opposite the client so as to have full view of his eye movements, directed at symbols placed round the edge of a large board. The board may either have a hole in the middle to permit viewing or be made of clear plastic.

Encoding

A board similar to the above may also be used for selection by means of encoding. Encoding techniques direct the 'conversant' to the selected item through a combination of signals in a specified pattern. One encoding technique assigns different items to colour-coded groups, and the client points first at one of the colours displayed on his board and then at the item from the group of that colour. A more abstract equivalent, placing high cognitive demands on the client, requires the co-ordinates of items on a separate communication board to be mapped out in terms of columns and rows. The board for eye-pointing at is used to establish the co-ordinates of the chosen item, which the 'conversant' then confirms by pointing at it.

As a technique, encoding has the merit of being quicker than scanning and often more accurate than direct selection, but the client needs sufficient cognitive ability to cope with (at least) two stages of encoding his choice. The two stages may, however, be very simple. For example, the client might spontaneously indicate one part of the house or a particular direction outside; at the second stage, he might respond to verbal scanning of likely items in a certain room or well-known spot nearby. This simple kind of two-stage strategy is typical of visual encoding techniques that handicapped people are naturally taught.

Combination Techniques

Direct selection, scanning and encoding can be used in any combination.

Gesture may indicate the need or desire to converse, after which another method can be used to specify the vocabulary. Direct selection of topic areas on a communication board may precede the scanning of particular items. Conversely, the first stage, accomplished with the help of a 'conversant', may be scanning to select one of several boards, sheets or colour-coded groups of items, and the second stage may be direct selection.

Equipment and Accessing

Most of the strategies we have been discussing can be implemented via a range of equipment. When this is technically advanced, it normally incorporates two elements, one of which produces and displays the components (i.e. in the present context, symbols) and the other which actually operates the equipment. Low-tech equipment does not always need the second element as the client using it is likely to play a larger physical part in communicating.

New devices are continually being developed, but although they may be more portable, attractive or readily acceptable, such innovations often represent only a refinement of the same basic style of implementation. Therefore, although our categories of device do not make up a complete catalogue of communication technology, they do include a large proportion of the basic designs for communication aids currently in use by multiply handicapped people.

The 'Attention-getter'

The term 'attention-getter' describes any aid which produces a simple alerting signal, such as a buzzer bell, computer-generated sound, etc. Attention-getters pass no specific message, but the manner in which they are used may demonstrate something of the user's emotions and the context may make clear his purpose in attracting a 'conversant's' attention. Switching mechanisms which can operate these devices are described later in the chapter.

Even if a person is grossly physically handicapped, usually some subtle form of alerting exists naturally. The advantage of an electric, electronic or mechanical attention-getter is that the signal can be magnified, making it easier for the conversant to pick up the signal. This is especially important in group educational settings so that a user can gain the teacher or therapist's attention even when she is not directly facing him.

Attention-getting devices can also be used to pinpoint an item during scanning or can confirm the correctness of a message after it has been interpreted by a 'conversant'.

Unfortunately, devices which produce bleeping, buzzing and so forth do share a general problem: they can become somewhat grating to people's sensibilities. Children in particular may overuse them, to the annoyance of families and teachers. Like telephones, they have a maddeningly demanding quality. There may also be a problem in locating the source of a sound when there are several users in one establishment. One solution is to arrange that each user's device gives out a different sound. However, the disadvantages of living with the simultaneous production of buzzing, bleeping and ringing are obvious.

The Communication Board

Communication boards which can serve both in conversation and instruction are rather quieter than attention-getters, more versatile and very popular. They may be constructed out of a range of materials, e.g. plywood, plastic or kitchen laminate. Important qualities are durability and lightness, to ensure easy portability.

Pictures, photographs and/or symbols can be mounted on a board to make up the vocabulary. Two distinct strategies allow items to be introduced one at a time: either each new item is attached at the time it is learned, or the full potential vocabulary is attached from the start but the items not yet learned are masked out. The latter option makes it easier to pre-plan the final location of items, but if the ultimate vocabulary is to be large it has the disadvantage of restricting the size of individual items. At the learning stage, clients may be helped by greater size. Pre-printed Bliss vocabularies keep the physical size of the chart constant and as the number of items increases so the size of each is reduced.

A suitable means should be sought of protecting the vocabulary from wear and tear, food and drink, and perhaps saliva if the client has difficulties in oral control. Common forms of protection are a transparent sheet of rigid perspex or of the clear sticky-back plastic available on rolls. The former must be specially cut to size and does not provide full protection from sideways seepage, but it can be lifted up if necessary so that the symbol array on the board underneath can be modified.

As mentioned above, boards designed for eye-pointing are wholly transparent, or in the shape of a hollow square, so the 'conversant' can see through to the client on the opposite side. Card items or even real objects can be attached to make up the vocabulary — though not so many that the 'conversant's' view of the user's eyes is obstructed. Items also need to be well spaced out because it is difficult to make fine distinctions in the direction of someone's gaze; it is important too that the user should be able to hold his gaze steady enough for its direction to be reasonably clear.

Many communication boards are mounted horizontally on a table which the client also uses for eating, working, etc. Another suitable site, if the board's dimensions permit, is the lap-tray of a wheelchair. Slightly tilting the board or tray may make for clearer viewing or easier use of a head pointer or other selection aid. Of course when tilted the board may present problems as a multi-purpose surface; on the other hand, when it is flat the symbols displayed on it can easily get obscured during practical activities.

Symbol Charts for the Mobile

Trying to stabilise a sturdy communication board while conversing with its help may be difficult for an active ambulant individual. A conventional board, even if a handle or slot makes it easy to carry, cannot be securely attached to a person as it can to a wheelchair and so it may tend to be left around. When fitted to a rollator or similar mobility aid it can be transported quite conveniently, but many physically handicapped individuals are mobile without recourse to any such aid. For someone who is independently ambulant despite, say, a hemiplegic condition, trying to stabilise a board with an affected arm and point with the other meanwhile is a clumsy method of communicating.

Active ambulant people need aids that are particularly compact, light and portable. To encompass a fairly large vocabulary, items can be organised within a concertina- or book-like format. A disadvantage for a mentally handicapped user is that searching through to locate the desired symbol requires patience, motivation and manual dexterity as well as a degree of cognitive competence. An alternative style of presentation is to display graphic symbols on the wall of a room. Large-size symbols can be clearly indicated. Naturally this is not a very portable method and the style of wallcovering may not appeal within the family home.

One novel location for displaying symbols is on garments. Items are stabilised when knitted into or printed on garments worn by the user or his 'conversant'. Possible disadvantages are some people's aversion to being prodded and the difficulty of seeing all the symbols on one's own clothes. Some women's clothing has the advantage that it can be raised for clearer viewing by both the 'conversant' and the user. While raising a skirt is perhaps not *de rigeuer* in polite society, raising a symbol-printed plastic apron is quite socially acceptable. Viewing will be easier if the apron is made of special material or given a backing so that it remains fairly still and flat.

Simple Electronic and Mechanical Aids

For clients who physically cannot cope with direct selection, there are numerous commercially available aids with units that can be lit up in scanning patterns. Control is through some form of switching mechanism (as discussed below). Usually scanning is from left to right, top to bottom, following the conventional reading pattern. Alternatively, if a dial display is used, a pointer can follow the sweeping pattern of a clock hand or a flashing light can travel round the dial. Many of the recently produced light-scanning aids have a memory facility: elements can remain fully or partially lit up after their initial selection (but see page 94 for a discussion of the possible linguistic disadvantages). This type of aid was illustrated in Figure 4.2.

Where a computer system is being used, the memorised vocabulary elements can be reproduced in sequence on a VDU.

Voice Synthesisers

One great disadvantage of communication aids which involve the use of a non-speech alternative is the difficulty of carrying on regular conversations with members of the community at large. An appealing solution is a device which accepts a visual symbol as input but produces a vocal output. No intelligent translation is involved, simply a match between the symbol position and the synthesised voice. The devices are produced as portable boxes with the surface arrangement of a small communication board. Each element can be programmed for the vocal output of a single word or longer phrase. Technical developments have greatly improved voice quality; usually this is now quite acceptable — a far cry from the old synthesisers whose monotones conjured up images of quite inhuman beings.

Voice synthesisers do not always satisfy communication needs. Some available devices are 'dedicated' — i.e. they cannot be flexibly reprogrammed in location if the client's increasing mastery of the system requires an altered or extended vocabulary. Also, quite apart from the linguistic or intellectual ability of the handicapped person, a visual array has inevitable limitations which can become apparent when a client wishes to use the system for conversation rather than the production of standard messages. Even if the synthesised conversation were to be grammatically regular, it would be well nigh impossible to programme in appropriate intonation patterns, as these transcend individual words.

Some versatile modern equipment has a reprogrammable memory of about 2000 words — far greater than the likely requirements of a mentally handicapped user. However, access to it is via spelling, not by the much more limited symbol array which is more accessible and better suited to a mentally handicapped clientele. Given only a limited number of symbols, the only way to enlarge the vocabulary is by the use of combine strategies. Special Bliss programmes do exist for the expression in a single word of some conventionally used symbol-compounds: for example, BOX + EAR + ELECTRICITY would be synthesised as RADIO. However, non-standard combines are still expressed according to their individual units, which may be difficult to interpret within the flow of a synthesised conversation.

At the present time, therefore, voice synthesisers for mentally handicapped users are perhaps better suited to the transmission of standard messages than to flexible conversational interchanges.

Interface Switching Mechanisms

No matter how versatile a piece of electronic equipment, or how ingenious a computer-assisted learning program, its practicality as a communicative aid is determined by its accessibility to potential users. This is largely governed by the means of access or switching mechanisms which form the interface between the user and the machine he is operating.

There are four basic models of switching, operated respectively by pressure or touch, voice or other sound, suck and/or blow and heat. Especially within the first category, there is a range of quite distinctive pieces of equipment. A few devices do not fall neatly into any of the above categories.

Switching devices operated by pressure or touch include the following:

— push buttons, including multiple keyboards (see also next section) and recessed buttons set into a board to prevent accidental operation;
— levers and paddles for rocking, tilting or pushing (see Figure 4.3);
— pillow or pad for punching or pressing;
— sliding switches for operating by hand and sliding foot 'trolleys';
— wobblestick which operates the switching mechanism when moved off-centre in any direction (see Figure 4.3);
— joystick which can be moved to certain predetermined positions, usually between two and eight (see Figure 4.3).

Some of the devices can give much more than the off/on/start/record function. For example, continuous pressure on a pressure pad may promote a graded response such as faster scanning and joysticks in use with a VDU may permit the scanning of an array of symbols in any direction. Mixed modal switching is also available, e.g. on the lines of hand-held television control devices, which involve both touch and some form of directed radiation.

Switch utility may not be dependent so much on its basic mode as on style of

Figure 4.3: Pressure and Touch Switching Devices

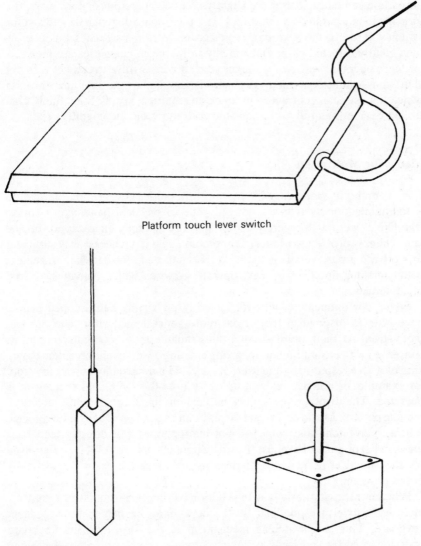

Platform touch lever switch

Wobblestick   Joystick

use and positioning. For instance, the touch mechanism known as a wobblestick can be calibrated to respond to the slightest sensation; the device, which incorporates a very long contact rod, can be successfully used by clients with severe athetoid conditions. Many pressure-pad switches can be mounted close to sensitive parts of a multiply handicapped person so that they can be operated by a mere jerk of the hand, foot, knee, etc.

Other switches may require even less gross physical involvement. Sucking or blowing on a tube can indicate a yes/no response, or blowing on a sensitive air paddle can cause it to move slightly so as to operate a switch. A whistle switch can be operated by the sound of an ultra-sonic dog-whistle and a voice switch will respond to a word or even a grunt. Infra-red switches are operable by a clearly directed gaze. Outside any of the given categories are moisture switches operated only by the tongue (they are insensitive to contact with dry skin) and switches operated via electrodes applied to the skin near muscles which the user can contract to produce an electrical signal. Such finely controlled devices naturally require some concentration and cognitive skill.

Media for Motivation

For a multiply handicapped person, difficulties of gaining access to a communication system are not only due to physical handicap: as those who live or work with severely and profoundly mentally handicapped people know, simply providing the means to communicate is not necessarily sufficient to motivate a passive client to do so. He may need further encouragement before making an effort to, say, operate a switch which activates a piece of equipment.

Some 'communication' aids for mentally/physically handicapped people have little to distinguish them from more general media for teaching and motivation. At their simplest, such aids include many computer programs concerned with basic stimulation, giving exciting positive reinforcement to any kind of active response by the user. On a VDU animals may appear in a zoo, for example, or a house be built up every time the switching mechanism is operated. The display may simply be flashing lights or a brightly coloured moving pattern. Music or a visual display can depend on vocalisation directed into a microphone and some special microphones will directly feed back the vocalisation they have just 'heard'. Some clients are sufficiently aroused by the practice of actively responding to move on to a linguistically based program.

Whether receiving early language tuition or simply a stimulating reinforcement for actively responding, these clients may be helped by a concept keyboard. This is a switching mechanism in the form of a flat keyboard operated by surface pressure. Associated computer programs allow it either to serve as a single large response area or to have the number of options extended upwards one at a time, in which case the size of each response area is concomitantly reduced. Keyboard overlays designed to correspond with the programs indicate switching areas. The fineness of discrimination required can be suited to a client's ability, as can the outcome of his response.

Many essentially sensation-producing devices have been designed especially to motivate children, e.g. the sound bubble, which is a plastic hemisphere with

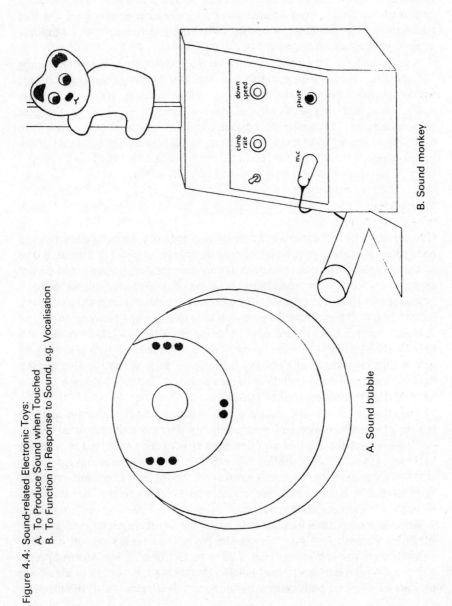

Figure 4.4: Sound-related Electronic Toys:
A. To Produce Sound when Touched
B. To Function in Response to Sound, e.g. Vocalisation

A. Sound bubble

B. Sound monkey

sensors arranged on it which emit a variable range of sounds when touched. A toy designed to encourage vocalisation is a monkey which climbs a stick in response to sounds made by the child. Both the above are illustrated in Figure 4.4.

Conventional mechanical or electronic toys can often be adapted quite easily for operation by a multiply handicapped child. Such stimulating items encourage him to respond actively and can also help to initiate concentration and study skills. If used appropriately, they can promote good posture (through careful positioning of the switching mechanism) and reinforce communicative social contact.

A snare to avoid, however, is getting hooked on novelty items while tending to forget that they are a means to an end. Much of the early computer software was sensation orientated; the hope must be that the client will learn to learn and so progress to specifically educational programs. Perhaps the best guarantee against becoming too wedded to a particular application is to keep in touch with other professionals working in the same field but in a variety of locations.

Conclusion

Our introduction to the vast and burgeoning growth of communication aids has been attempted through a series of classifications: of style, of format and of switching mode. The classifications are in the main explanatory and do not aspire to the clinical or educational function of determining clients' needs.

In fact with the advance of technology our categories sometimes break down — with practical benefits to the user. For example, the line between direct and indirect selection blurs if we equate an arrow moved on a VDU by means of a joystick with a directly pointed finger. Certainly some blow-switching devices can be directly pointed at a display (see Figure 4.5). We might also ask if a heat-operated infra-red switching device counts as indirect selection or as a form of direct selection akin to eye-pointing.

The progressive blurring of the distinction between communication aids and teaching programs is also beneficial to clients. Tuition in the use of an aid has always been needed and this has often been an educative and mind-broadening experience in itself. Now, the flexibility that computerisation brings may mean that the form and scope of communication software will alter, and indeed be programmed to change, in direct response to a client's success as he follows through a graded teaching program.

Anyone who wishes to keep abreast of the latest developments must be prepared to comb regularly through the pages of at least some of the many journals on micro-technology (e.g. *Learning to Cope: Computers in Special Education*) for the present pace of innovation does not lend itself to the slower process of planned publication, let alone detailed research. Exhibitions of

Figure 4.5: Blow-operated Direct Selection Keyboard

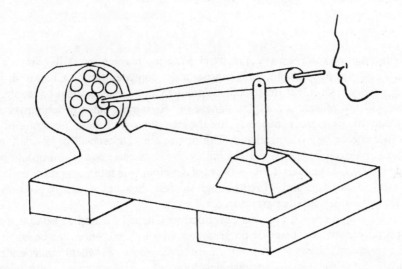

technological aids also allow professionals and lay people to find out about recent ideas and try out new devices. Even if no independent assessment of their potential value is available, such opportunities are a useful way of extending one's knowledge.

(Readers wishing for more background knowledge of micro-technology and its application to mentally handicapped people are recommended to read the compactly presented *Microcomputers and Special Educational Needs: A Guide to Good Practice* by Bob Hogg (1984). Although a few details are already dated, it is a sympathetic and very informative survey. See also *Micros for Handicapped Users* (Saunders 1984). Information about methods of symbol display and switching mechanisms is to be found in *Handbook to Blyssymbolics* (Silverman *et al.* 1978). On a regular regional basis information is compiled in the UK by the Special Education Micro Electronics Resource Centres — SEMERCs.

Details on some suppliers of communication aids are included in Appendix C.)

5   TEACHING NON-SPEECH COMMUNICATION

This chapter explores ways of improving the communication skills of mentally handicapped people who, unlike those under consideration in Chapter 4, are physically able. It will aim to provide pointers and stimulate ideas on teaching, but will not present a complete language programme since programmes are obtainable from other sources. After the introductory section, the choice of an initial vocabulary is considered. The rest of the chapter will be divided into three main sections: 'In the Beginning' is concerned with the initiation of language, 'On the Way' looks at ways of developing greater awareness and use of simple language and 'Making Progress' describes techniques for promoting language which is more structured.

Of the non-speech systems described in Chapters 2 and 3, several have specially associated teaching programmes, to which references can be found in the relevant sections. As an alternative, some excellent independent programmes for speech/language development can be adapted to incorporate a non-speech system. The following are examples: *The First Words Language Programme* (Gillham 1979), followed by *Two Words Together: A First Sentences Language Programme* (Gillham 1983); *Wessex Revised Portage Language Checklist* (White and Earl 1983); *Derbyshire Language Scheme Teaching Manual* (Knowles and Masidlover 1979).

While up till now the differing characteristics of the different systems and types of system have been highlighted, the present authors believe that there are times when a synthesis of systems opens doors, maintaining options for learning and expression as well as allowing flexibility in teaching across a broad spectrum of approaches. A dichotomy between signs and symbols is unnecessary, for the one can reinforce the other and either can lead towards speech. Even different systems within the same mode may not be mutually exclusive: a simpler system may facilitate the learning of a more complex one and cross-fertilisation may germinate new ideas. This view of the essential unity of the many alternative systems pervades our thinking in the teaching context.

Since the present chapter is concerned with teaching, all those who are learning signs and symbols will be referred to as 'students', whether they are young children, adolescents or adults. By the same token, any teaching adult — parent, teacher, nurse, speech therapist, etc. — will be referred to as a 'teacher'. Naturally, 'teachers' will wish to adapt some of the teaching methods described to suit their own situation. For convenience, 'students' and 'teachers' of either sex will be referred to as male and female respectively.

Initial Vocabulary

There is general agreement on the need to restrict initial vocabulary. The precise number of words will vary according to students' abilities, but it should be small enough to allow ample opportunity for repetition and reinforcement.

Selection of vocabulary is influenced by several factors, of which we shall touch on the following:

— developmental readiness;
— frequency of usage by young (normal) children;
— usefulness to the student;
— non-conceptual influences on learning;
— (with reference to signs) ease of execution.

A teacher's choice of vocabulary for her students should not lie beyond what her students are developmentally ready to learn — in parallel to the natural vocabulary selection of developmentally normal children. Only as they grow in maturity and experience does their vocabulary progress beyond simple, familiar and concrete concepts to anything more complex and abstract. Experiments using symbols (Cregan 1980; House, Hanley and Magid 1980) support the theory that ease of learning is largely determined by the nature of the referent (i.e. the object or other concept that is referred to by the symbol — or sign or word). The most easily learned are those which are well within the cognitive grasp of the student.

Core vocabularies for signs or symbols can be drawn from lists compiled by analysis of the spoken vocabulary of young normal children. From among these, Gillham's *First Words Language Programme* (1979) has already been mentioned. A vocabulary geared to early sign learning has been compiled by two American authors: Fristoe and Lloyd's 'Initial Expressive Sign Lexicon for Persons with Severe Communication Impairment' (1980) is a conveniently basic list, though other students following early language programmes, as the authors recognise, may have additional or slightly different needs. The lexicon, which contains only about 70 items, is interesting in its concentration on expression. The vocabulary of the Sigsymbol system (Cregan 1982) expands Fristoe and Lloyd's lexicon with special reference to a school setting and to additional 'educational' receptive language.

Many teachers believe strongly in the importance of including words (i.e. signs or symbols) which particularly appeal to or interest individual students. For example, different words are functional for students who are home-based and those living in a larger residential establishment. One student may have a special interest in his pet rabbits, another in cars, clothes or his special diet. A student's customary environment will influence the most relevant choice, and words which *he* sees as functional, that is those which bring about a result he desires or enjoys, can be useful in their power to motivate.

It is not only the underlying concepts of signs or symbols that affect how easily they are learned but other properties too (Karlan and Lloyd 1983). Iconicity is one property that assists learning. Another is distinctiveness: easy to discriminate seems to mean easy to learn. Two signs/symbols which resemble each other are more difficult to remember, even if, say, greater complexity in signing is involved. Regarding signs alone, those which require familiar or easily reproduced hand postures are most readily used; signs for one hand are preferred to those for two, and where two hands are used symmetrical signs (i.e. two hands the same) are found easier than asymmetrical. On the whole users show a preference for signs involving touch, where the hands touch each other or another part of the body.

Acquisition of an initial vocabulary such as we have been discussing is a long-term goal for many severely mentally handicapped students. At the very start, to have learnt a single sign is a major achievement and teaching strategy is all important.

In the Beginning

Among the most difficult students to teach are those whose communication problems are accompanied by problem behaviour. Typical descriptions are 'hyperactive' or 'non-communicating' and they are often unresponsive to verbal or any other form of communication. Stereotyped behaviours are common, such as obsessive hand-flapping, finger-drumming or head-rolling, which make full attention to a set task impossible.

For these students, and for any who have great difficulty in concentrating, pre-training is essential. Behavioural methods, as described in the introduction, have proved to be the most effective way of extinguishing these blocks to learning. Some teachers may deliver negative reinforcement whenever undesirable behaviours occur. Much more directly productive is the use of systematic positive reinforcement to establish a student's willingness to sit down at a table and attend for even a second or two to a stimulus chosen by the teacher. At this point the main training programme can begin.

A Behavioural Programme

The behavioural training technique is illustrated below by an elaboration of part of Jones' (1979) programme for teaching the correspondence between a symbol APPLE and a real (piece of) apple.

Choice of Reinforcer.   It was ascertained that the child liked eating apples, so a piece of apple could function as a positive reinforcer.

Objective Stated in Behavioural Terms. 'The child will request a piece of apple by placing the appropriate symbol on the tray provided. He will do this without error on ten consecutive occasions in a teaching session.'

Task Analysis.   A step-by-step sequence of teaching goals might be as follows (note that each one is also stated in behavioural terms):

(1) 'Having been encouraged to examine the whole apple and watch it being cut up, the child will pick up a piece of apple from the table in front of him and eat it. He will do this on ten consecutive occasions in a teaching session.'
(2) 'With a physical prompt, the child will pick up a symbol-card APPLE from beside a piece of apple on the table and place it on an adjacent tray. He will then be allowed to eat the apple. He will do this on ten consecutive occasions in a teaching session.'
(3) 'The child will follow the procedure in (2), but prompts will be faded as he learns to respond independently.'

(Note that this sequence of learning is errorless, as prompts are only faded when the child is able to respond correctly.)

Schedule of Reinforcement.   While the new behaviour was being established, the child received the piece of apple as a reward on every occasion that he performed correctly – i.e. since the learning was errorless, on every single occasion. The schedule was one of continuous reinforcement.

(Note that although regular reinforcement is vital for sustaining motivation, in some situations non-edible rewards may be preferable but difficult to find. One escape route from this problem is described by Reid and Hurlbut (1977), in whose project students learned to communicate by pointing to pictures of well-liked leisure areas, being reinforced by a visit to their chosen area.)

Assessment/Recording.   Assessment would entail observing the number of responses in each training session and recording would note how many sessions were required before prompts could be faded and before the child could respond quite independently. If the child tired easily, the programme might be modified to require only five correct responses as the criterion for successfully achieving each goal. Recording would also enable the teacher to compare the child's speed of learning the symbol-apple correspondence with his speed of learning the next similar task, and so permit his progress to be precisely monitored. Not the least important reason for this is to encourage the teacher by clearly identifying progress.

Some readers may feel that this section has gone into unnecessarily fine detail. In justification we would reply that a clear understanding of the behavioural technique is essential for systematic teaching of early language skills to a mentally handicapped student whose language is severely impaired. This is not to deny that at a later stage social interaction and freer game-based activities have an equally important part to play, and that at all times the teacher should attempt to form a real relationship with the student.

Early Learning

A number of students may never acquire more than a very few functional words relating to their immediate needs, each one a reinforcer in its own right. One study (Murphy, Steele, Gilligan, Yeow and Spare 1977) details the choice of PEANUTS, DRINK, SWEETS, COMB and TOOLS, which were represented by pictures. If the child chose COMB he had his hair combed and if he chose TOOLS he was allowed to bang nails into wood with a hammer. They found that TOOLS were rarely chosen, but that PEANUTS and DRINK were very popular. The present authors have found that SWIMMING is another popular word and in fact know one deaf autistic girl who has learned to use that sign and no other.

Opinions differ as to whether PLEASE as a general request should be taught. Some practitioners feel that students may be confused because it is not attached to a specific referent, but the authors have not found this to be the case. They know a number of children who have learned to sign PLEASE appropriately through being systematically prompted to do so in appropriate situations, even when the same children have scant knowledge of other signs. Its use certainly increases a student's social acceptability and a sharp reminder to 'say please' can at times act surprisingly well as a control when edibles might otherwise be grabbed without finesse.

In the above situation, speech serves to prompt a sign. In other situations a teacher may find signing is a useful alternative to physical prompting. When, for example, a student is uncertain of the correct choice of symbol from an array – perhaps he is being asked to choose the symbol for DRINK before being allowed to have his mid-morning drink – the teacher has to decide on the most suitable method of prompting. If she physically guides the student's hand or points to the symbol he should select, he may act co-operatively but in fact pay little attention to what he is doing. But, if he is to learn and remember, his active attention is vital. Choosing the symbol in response to a sign means that he has actively processed the cue, transferring his understanding from one mode to another.

Signs have also been used to facilitate word-object association (Bricker 1972). Children were taught to imitate signs, if necessary with physical prompting, then to pair them with the spoken words and then to pair the same signs with the objects. It was found that many children learned by this method to associate the words with the objects, though some did so very much more quickly than others.

An interesting comparison can be made with the subject of Murphy *et al.*'s (1977) research (the boy who liked peanuts). This boy followed Bricker and Bricker's (1970) behavioural training programme and learned to imitate signs, but completely failed to comprehend their association with word-meaning, even after a large number of training sessions. In contrast, he learned a basic 'picture language' vocabulary with relative ease. Teachers are well advised to learn from these examples that, even when training methods are known to be effective, a student's innate aptitude can have a radical effect, for better or worse, on what he manages to learn. When planned and systematic teaching has led only to failure, it makes good sense to experiment with other approaches.

Whatever the approach, the progress of 'difficult' or unco-operative students is often bedevilled by poor attention. Observation usually shows that they are capable of attention, but direct it to objects and activities of their own choice rather than the teacher's. However, when there are several modes of input using stimuli which correspond to each other (words, signs and symbols) via more than one sensory channel, there may be less room for distractions. It is also possible that the multiple input may help to combat the over-selective attention of autistic students (Gersten 1980).

All students are affected by whether or not they find the teaching situation congenial. Above all, a good relationship between teacher and student helps to draw the student's attention in the right direction — just as a mother and her child first forge an inter-personal link, and then with 'intersubjectivity of attention' together look at the world outside (Trevarthan and Hubley 1978).

On the Way

Many students who have acquired the rudiments of language still lack motivation to make use of their skill. They may have a facility for 'switching off' or withdrawing from a group situation, though they are not at all disruptive. Possibly they are not averse to contact with adults, but rarely go out of their way to seek it. Without overt disturbance, individuals may deliberately resist being taught. Alternatively, teaching difficulties can stem from their passivity.

Structured one-to-one teaching is obviously often necessary for students with disordered behaviour, as successful teaching of a whole group to some extent presupposes that individual members are willing to co-operate and attend. On the other hand, students who are prepared to sit as part of a group, even if their attention is somewhat intermittent, may benefit from teaching directed at others. In a classroom, management of other students while an individual is receiving one-to-one tuition can be an ongoing problem; in such a setting, the group set-up has much to recommend it.

Another factor to consider is instanced by Chris, a young adolescent with emotional problems in addition to his mental handicap. Chris would only consent to learn when he could pretend he was not listening. He countered direct instruction by an averted face and occasional outbursts of chair-throwing, but if the teacher kept her interaction with him very low-key he would demonstrate that he had in fact been learning while other members of the group were being taught. There were also social benefits in his being a group member, for if other students took the initiative he permitted himself occasional interaction with them.

'Real-life' Learning

With a relatively amenable group of students, it becomes feasible to teach some sign/symbol concepts through 'real-life' experience, though structured language experience outside the classroom makes high demands on staffing resources. Opportunities for the introduction of new signs/symbols arise in many regularly occurring situations – getting up, washing, eating, drinking, going outdoors, tidying up, watching television, etc. – where the language is embedded in a meaningful context. Play inside and out of the classroom can be structured to mesh with language teaching. It is important that students do not associate the meaning and use of signs and symbols with a single context only.

Some settings lend themselves to having a permanent display of appropriate symbols, for example around the classroom and at strategic points in the grounds (on the seat, the swings, the gate and so on). As an alternative, symbols can be produced ready-made by a teacher or even drawn on the spot as the students watch. A symbol can be placed or tapped on the object it represents and the word spoken; students can be encouraged to follow suit. Signing can provide an additional linguistic dimension, cued by the context, with or without an accompanying symbol and/or a prompt from the teacher. Teaching contexts can be planned and structured into the day's routine, e.g. playing with a dog, driving in a car or minibus, visiting a shop, so that vocabulary can be gradually extended.

The word 'gradually' is important, for we are not recommending an indiscriminate enrichment programme, either of the kind advocated at one time by nursery schools or that followed by the deaf-blind but intelligent Helen Keller, where in order to instil the vital concept that 'everything has a name', anything and everything in the little girl's experience was named to her (Keller 1966). As discussed in Chapter 1 (and see Fenn 1976), for a person who is mentally handicapped this kind of broad enrichment is more likely to cause confusion than facilitate learning. However, even if the so-called 'poor memory' of mentally handicapped students makes it essential to put strict limits on earliest vocabulary, later on the 'learning to learn' phenomenon may considerably extend possibilities.

In fact research (e.g. Butterfield, Wambold and Belmont 1973) indicates that once learning has taken place, the long-term memory of mentally handicapped people is not impaired; the real deficit is directly related to difficulties of mental organisation and rehearsal. In an attempt to overcome these, the teacher's organisation of material is crucial. The behavioural framework with its small logical steps remains an effective model, even if some learning activities are introduced which are freer and more experimental.

One approach to early learning greatly enjoyed by young children focuses on actions rather than objects and, though classroom based, involves the children in a 'real' activity. It concentrates on receptive understanding. Following the cue for a verb such as RUN, SIT or JUMP, children carry out the action, assisted as necessary by the teacher. The same cues occur several times in one session for frequent repetition is an essential part of the learning process. Correct responses from the children are reinforced verbally and socially, but the activity itself also forms its own reward.

Playing Games

Table games are helpful in extending and reinforcing sign/symbol learning, provided other experience backs up the links with real life. They can also provide a good opportunity for social interaction and let students have the pleasurable and very motivating experience of controlling someone else's behaviour.

A very simple game involves a few items of clothing, such as gloves, hat and scarf. Students take turns to make a sign signifying a particular garment or to show the corresponding symbol to their neighbour, who must select and put on that garment. Adult assistance may of course be necessary, both for giving the instruction and carrying it out. Using language for the purpose of control as well as having to conform in the taking of turns are valuable aspects of social learning.

A rather more complex game sets up interchanges which can be directly generalised to everyday situations. Students learn to make requests, accede to them and thank each other. Each student has one or two common objects in front of him (e.g. bunch of keys, toothbrush, etc.) and an array of matching noun-symbols is placed in the centre of the table. The student making the request holds a card strip which reads PLEASE in symbol form, followed by an empty space, and chooses one of the noun-symbols to fill the empty space. He either shows this request directly to the holder of the matching object or uses it to cue a signed request. The object-holder replies, cued by a card strip which reads YES or YOU CAN, and hands over the object. The recipient thanks him with the help of a symbol THANK YOU. This game can be followed immediately by the distribution of biscuits or drinks, carrying out the very same procedures in a real-life situation as in the game.

Even if competitiveness in games is a concept that many students do not understand, they may be motivated by the satisfaction of playing games requiring the completion of a task. It is easier to appreciate the achievement of, say, filling a lotto base-board than to understand the abstract concept of 'winning'. One lotto variant requires the matching of a symbol to a picture or vice versa; in another, the teacher gives out a card only in response to the appropriate sign from a student. Posting a card is another satisfying 'completion'. Students take it in turns to request a card from the teacher by sign, by speech or by selecting its pair. Only correct matching or requesting is rewarded by the student being allowed to post the card. (A slotted postbox is a piece of equipment easily made from an empty cardboard carton.)

Autistic students may find especial difficulties with the cross-modal coding in these games, where a stimulus in one mode requires a response in a different one. The findings of some researchers (e.g. Hobson and Duncan 1979) indicate that a word plus a picture elicits signs better than either word or picture on its own. Other findings (see Kotkin, Simpson and Desanto 1978) suggest that presenting a sign along with the spoken word seems to facilitate the learning of the word as a label for a picture/symbol. Different presentations can be tried out by the teacher to establish if one is significantly easier than another for particular students, with obvious implications for their future teaching.

Expression and Meaning

Most students have some understanding of language before they learn to express themselves. This is the developmental pattern of normal children, in which receptive language precedes expressive. Agreement is not, however, universal that this is necessarily the most effective teaching order for mentally handicapped people. Some research by Smeets and Striefel (1976) suggests that the physical expression of signs contributes to receptive learning; in their study, simply learning to 'read' signs did not help the subjects to express them. Buckley (1984), in her work with Down's children, draws parallel conclusions. Her findings are that (1) a rote-learned vocabulary may subsequently become meaningful in the right teaching context; and (2) some children may go straight from the visual form of the word to its meaning (e.g. reading out the written word 'closed' as 'shut'). Bearing in mind these findings, teachers may at times decide to concentrate on eliciting expressive responses and at a later stage 'add on' the meaning through further teaching.

In the authors' experience, this approach worked well with one young man, David. David had strong likes and dislikes of certain foods, e.g. jelly beans and cheese respectively. He would accept the former by grabbing and eagerly vocalising; the latter he would reject with a squawk and wildly waving arms. In lotto games he was taught by rote (Makaton) signs for the (Sig) symbols YES and NO. In one-to-one sessions he was then offered jelly beans or morsels of cheese and cued by symbols to sign his acceptance or rejection of them according to his known preferences. As David learned how to respond to the offers, symbol cues were faded. If by mistake he gave the 'wrong' answer, he was horrified to have the jelly bean taken away from him or the cheese thrust upon him!

With further practice, David came to generalise the use of 'yes' and 'no' to food offered at mealtimes, though never to more abstract situations like going to the toilet. Nor did he learn to answer appropriately when asked if he had understood something, or to indicate non-comprehension in any way, a skill which would have been most useful to teacher and taught. He did, however, become better motivated overall; his readiness to apply himself increased and he showed signs of learning to learn.

When behaviour and motivation improve in the course of a non-speech language programme, the change may be attributable to the new acquisition of language, the regular and systematic teaching or the generally increased amount of attention. In any case, progress may be greater than anticipated, so that teaching goals and methods may need to be modified accordingly.

Making Progress

The majority of students who make good progress are likely to have reasonable cognitive ability and social awareness, and to have acquired enough receptive language to follow simple instructions. Expressive language, signed or spoken, may be limited, but a start will have been made.

In class groups, one or more members may have quite good speech, but for a number of reasons this need not be a deterrent to introducing a non-speech programme. Firstly, one student who speaks may help to stimulate others to do the same. Secondly, if a speaker learns the expressive (sign) language of his peers he will be able to understand them. Thirdly, non-speech alternatives may mediate towards further improvements in a speaker's communication skills. Fourthly, he may benefit by acquiring other peripheral skills.

Andrew, an adolescent with fluent speech, was one student who received spin-off benefits peripheral to the main programme. He had considerable difficulties in physical co-ordination and, until he participated in a signing programme, was quite unable to imitate even very simple hand positions. For the clasped hands of the Paget Gorman Sign System (PGSS) sign PLEASE, for example, he would stretch out and wave his arms in all directions and contort himself. With regular practice, his ability to observe and imitate progressed slowly but appreciably, to the point where he could make recognisable approximations unaided and his teacher noted an overall improvement in perceptual-motor co-ordination. Another speaking student who benefited from a non-speech programme was Nicola. Her words tended to be over-hasty and garbled, but she learned to control her rate of production through reading sentences in symbol form, pointing to each symbol as she spoke the word.

Linguistic Form

If students have acquired an initial vocabulary and can use communication purposefully, it is time to pay closer attention to linguistic form. At this stage, learning to cope with relatively complex combinations of signs/symbols/

words becomes a realistic goal, though one which many students find difficult to achieve. The rest of this section therefore focuses on the promotion of multi-word 'utterances'.

We have found that the repeated practice of simple and specific sentence forms may encourage students to generate their own similar sentences and use them spontaneously. In line with common early utterances of young children, it has proved practical and convenient to work on subject/verb and subject/verb/object strings. Because of the increased cognitive demands of prepositional concepts, students often find it more difficult to produce sentences containing a preposition. If the emphasis is semantic (i.e. concerned with meaning), then it is appropriate to omit verb inflections and the articles 'a' and 'the'. The form of eliciting questions can be varied, but each one must demand active processing by the student. For example, not only different information, but also different amounts of it are required according to the question asked, as illustrated by the following:

(1)   '*Who*('s) running?'
The only new information that the student must contribute is the subject. He must seek this from whatever further stimulus was coupled with the question. The further stimulus might be a man-doll made to run by the teacher – a particularly flexible type of stimulus, involving concrete and easily repeatable activity. Alternative stimuli include:
— a real man running
— a picture of a man running
— a story about a running man (more difficult unless accompanied by pictures)
— a television picture of a man running
— a computer-generated running stick figure.
The question may be spoken and signed and require a signed response. As an alternative, symbols may be indicated alongside the spoken word. If pointed to sequentially on a communication board, care is needed to ensure that *both* words are included in the reply. The question may be written down in symbol form or individual symbol cards set out in order.

When teaching Sigsymbols, we have often utilised a strip of card divided into sections on which to place the symbols, as in Figure 5.1. The student must pick up the correct noun-card for the subject (which could either be the only card available or chosen from an array) and position it in the empty section on the strip. The student then points to the symbols in the correct order and signs or attempts to speak the words.

(2)   'Man('s) doing *what*?'/'*What*('s) the man doing?'
The verb is the new information that must be sought this time. Teachers must decide on the most suitable word order when asking this question, whether signed, spoken or in symbol form, bearing in mind that the answer required

Figure 5.1: Sigsymbol Sentence Strips: Question to be Answered by Appropriate Placing of Individual Symbol-card

WHO'S RUNNING?

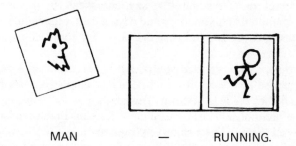

MAN   —   RUNNING.

is the subject followed by the verb. Even if the first question deviates from normal English usage, it has the advantage of preserving the subject/ verb order.

(3) *'Who*('s) doing *what?'*
The amount of information demanded by this question is precisely doubled; the level of difficulty it presents to the student largely depends on the reason for his not previously producing two-word 'utterances'. If this was mainly a difficulty in just getting the words together, it may well have been eased by practice in answering questions (1) and (2).

Alternatively, there may be a deeper cognitive problem in attending to two dimensions – the agent and the action – of the one situation. An approach that may help is to give practice in focusing on and labelling several dimensions of other stimuli (e.g. colour, shape, size, composition and function of an object). The aim is to make attention to more than one dimension habitual. Practice is also needed in sifting out what information is relevant to the question in hand.

One sociable young boy, Simon, had production problems. Single words (which he often signed to cue himself to speak) came easily, but were never combined without an intermediary prompt from an adult. This production problem was tackled by a procedure which limited the cognitive demands to a minimum at the same time as eliciting combinations of words. Pictures of noun pairs (e.g. cup and saucer, bat and ball) were named by Simon as the teacher pointed at them. A Sigsymbol AND was then placed below the picture and, assisted by pointing, Simon learnt to sign/say 'cup – and – saucer'. After further practice, he came to respond with the appropriate three-word phrase even in the absence of the AND symbol. He then moved on to more cognitively demanding combinations.

Such combinations included basic requests like 'Please go toilet' and 'Please have biscuit'. When learning to speak these, Simon also derived support from signs and symbols. He had great difficulty both in remembering all three words and in sequencing them correctly. To help him, several frequently-needed requests were drawn out in symbol form and permanently displayed in the classroom. Simon, with obvious pleasure, would select whichever was relevant, 'reading' it to sign and speak the words, until they were finally committed to his memory and he could utter the sentences without support. At this point, he began to use two-word and three-word sentences in spontaneous conversation.

In an experiment with retarded adults, House, Hanley and Magid (1980) had them compose sentences from individual symbols to describe actions which dolls had been made to perform. The adults' strategy was first to choose symbols in the order of salience of meaning (i.e. nouns first, prepositions last) and only then set them out according to syntactic rules. Such instances might indicate that, for those who have difficulty in organising and remembering sequences, a series of ready-sequenced symbol strings might be a practical alternative to conventional communication boards – at least when the use of sequences is only just beginning. As cues for expression in another modality, the strings make exact repetition possible, the student being able to process each step at his own pace, to the point where the whole sequence is understood, learned and internalised.

Later on, as stringing becomes habitual, ready-prepared symbol sentences hinder rather than promote expression, because they deter flexible and creative combinations. At this stage, for symbol users, communication boards on the Bliss-board model are preferable (whichever graphic system is being used), and students who sign are no longer dependent on cues.

Students can practise making up their own symbol combinations with individual symbols. A student taught by one of the authors had a tendency to echolalia (i.e. speech which echoes that of other people, having little or no meaning). He became much more aware of word-to-meaning correspondence when he had to analyse it to translate it into symbol form. While a student is concentrating on meaning, the teacher can help by controlling the structure. To do this, she should group symbols in sets according to parts of speech (perhaps further separating transitive and intransitive verbs, for still greater control). The sets should then be offered in an appropriate order (e.g. nouns, transitive verbs, nouns, or nouns intransitive verbs, prepositions, nouns). The student must actively scan each set in turn to select symbols to construct a meaningful sentence. Being offered one set at a time enables him to work step by step.

Reading Skills

Symbols bring the reading experience within the grasp of many students unable to cope with Traditional Orthography (TO). They also open up reading-based opportunities for teaching.

Work cards can be prepared in symbol form, the level and number of instructions being geared to individual ability. With practice, students may be able to follow them quite independently of the teacher. Tasks can initially be short and simple — 'Put a cross on the cars' (to be distinguished from people or animals), 'Circle the shapes which are *not* blue', 'Draw a line under all the figure 2s', and so on. At a later stage, cards can bear a full set of instructions, e.g. for making toast or a cup of tea. Simple recipes can be written out for students to follow with decreasing amounts of supervision. A series of work cards covering assignments for the day can be given to able students; they might have the freedom to choose the order of assignments, each one being approved by the teacher before they proceed to the next.

For expressive reading, 'personalised' stories can provide special motivation and can be based on actual events. Even the simplest stories appeal to the reader who figures as the 'hero' or 'heroine' of them, e.g.:

'Janet buys ice-cream.
Janet eats ice-cream.
Now ice-cream gone.'

or

'Tim runs.
Tim falls.
Tim cries.'

Questions can encourage prediction of what will happen next or emphasise the cause-and-effect through-line.

If students cannot at first recognise the spelled form of their own names, a distinctive personal symbol can be added, for example a brightly coloured geometric shape. Identification of the spelled word can be learned in association with the shapes, which can be cut out in card and worn for a time as badges or pendents.

Longer but still simple stories can be a good focus for practising expressive language, provided that the attention and cognitive development of the group are up to them. One approach with signing students is to elicit a signed description of a sequence of pictures. Teachers should note that the verbs often point up the story-line, so noun-labelling alone is insufficient. A similar story-centred approach using symbols would involve a ready-prepared selection on individual cards which could be arranged to form descriptive phrases or sentences. An alternative but related approach involves whole-sentence strips which the teacher shuffles for the student to arrange in sequential order, with or without the help of pictures.

Another method has been used successfully by one of the present authors, arousing the enthusiastic participation of small groups. Prior to the lesson, a story is composed consisting of a few short sentences. Grids of boxes, one for each word in each sentence, are drawn out. For the sake of clarity, each sentence can appear on a single sheet of paper. In the lesson, symbols (Sigsymbols in the original experiments) are drawn to make up the story, while the students watch and attempt to guess the meaning of each one, by signing or speech, before it is completed. (As well as story-reading, this gives practice in visual closure, which is a beneficial exercise for students with perceptual problems.)

Once the whole story is complete, students take it in turns to read out the sentences and are encouraged to discuss and answer questions on the story, to extend comprehension and reinforce vocabulary learning. Both more and less able students seem to enjoy watching the symbols being drawn and are motivated to read, even if they do not all follow the thread of a longer story.

Pages of stories written in this way can be stapled together and the stories tape-recorded. Students can then listen again to the stories while following them in the home-made books.

Conversation

When students begin to express themselves spontaneously, teachers' skills must be directed towards extending conversation. The tentative overtures of some students are easily overwhelmed or cut short by too quick or even *too* enthusiastic a response. A student needs time to gather his thoughts; he must also have confidence that what he is 'saying' (by sign, symbols or speech) is being attended to. The questioning face of the listener assures him that he is receiving the desired attention and is also an excellent non-verbal prompt for him to continue.

The teacher's responses must be carefully chosen so as to invite the development of a real conversation with several interchanges. The questions she asks should demand real answers and not be mere requests that the student should repeat information that the teacher plainly knows already. For example, it is better to ask 'Where is your friend?' or 'What did you have for breakfast?' than 'What colour is this mug?' She should also be wary of over-hasty repetition of her question; a little more processing time may be all the student needs – and seeing the questioning face which continues to seek his participation.

It is often difficult to avoid questions that lead to yes/no answers, but different phrasing should be used if possible. One such question tends to be followed by another and the teacher ends up talking far more than the student. Moreover, this kind of one-word response fails to stretch the student's powers of expression and he is not stimulated to try his hardest. To underestimate his powers does him no service.

Of all the factors which go towards stimulating conversation, the most important and effective arise from a teacher's personal qualities: a friendly and sensitive awareness, a good relationship with her students and the ability to create a secure environment in which people trust and are trusted. And indeed the very same applies at the level of even the most basic and rudimentary attempts at communication.

6 SUMMING UP

In the introduction we traced the confluence of interest in and initatives on behalf of mentally handicapped people that took place in the 1970s, with especial reference to the UK. The resultant development in alternative forms of communication has been the focus of the rest of this book, in which we have described some individual non-speech systems, their use and associated teaching methods. In this final chapter, we attempt some kind of summing up, through an overall comparison between sign systems and symbol systems, a consideration of the optimum teaching setting and a look at possible ways forward in the future.

Sign versus Symbols

Advantages and Disadvantages of Signing

The unique advantage of signing stems from its naturalness as an extension of natural gesture and non-specific body language. No aids of any sort are required by a signing person; in other words, signing systems are completely portable. The signer's hands are always with him to express needs or feelings of the moment and – provided only that he can recall the sign – there is no question of what vocabulary may be available. It is a very immediate form of communication and promotes direct social interaction. Some may assert, with good reason, that no disadvantages can outweigh the strength of this advantage.

Signing is achieved through relatively gross bodily movements, engaging the signer in a very concrete way. This active involvement of the body as well as the mind is likely to assist learning.

An able person communicating with a mentally handicapped signer usually uses speech and signing together, implicitly acknowledging the status of signing. The joint use also serves as a model for the handicapped person to imitate and so helps to encourage speech. The continual practice of motor imitation may stimulate additional vocal imitation and will certainly not impede it.

On the debit side, signing inevitably occupies the hands, so that practical activities and communication cannot be carried on simultaneously. Some would view signing with disfavour because it cannot automatically be understood by the uninitiated, for, though some signs are iconic and easily guessable, many are, or appear to be, arbitrary. (The heavily iconic Amer-Ind is something of an exception to this.) So signing may appear as bizarre or even threatening behaviour, which further distances mentally handicapped people from the rest of society.

Just as the quality of people's speech varies widely, even among the 'normal' population, so does quality of signing. Like speech, signing can be sloppily performed and incoherent at times. It too places certain physical demands upon the user which he may find difficult to meet, even when trying his hardest – which not all mentally handicapped signers are motivated to do.

There are other parallels between the characteristics of signing and speech that in the present context may be seen as disadvantages. Their transitory nature means that the receiver must be on hand and attending at the moment of production. (This is the other side of the coin to the very desirable immediacy of interaction.) Although it is possible for an able person to produce single signs/words for a client to affirm or reject, this does not emulate a full static array of symbols for visual scanning; in effect, both signing and speech depend on the client's power of recall, which is more taxing than simple recognition.

Whether or not the word order and syntax of speech are mirrored by the signing system, the sequencing of words/signs has to take place internally before being expressed. A client with deficits in short-term memory may find this a deterrent to word-stringing and to even mildly complex expression.

As we commented in Chapter 1, fluent signing requires regular practice and some commitment on the part of those caring for and communicating with the mentally handicapped person. In some environments, such a demand might be difficult to meet.

Advantages and Disadvantages of Using a Symbol System

On turning to symbols, we find no equivalent to the special relationship between signing and natural gesture. Nevertheless, symbol systems do have certain advantages, some of which directly reflect the disadvantages of signing.

No physical dexterity is required in order to communicate by symbols. Even for direct selection, pointing will suffice, either with a finger or with a pointer attached to any movable part of the body. At their physical simplest, symbols can serve to convey a message with no more than the tiniest signal of affirmation from the client, given technical assistance in scanning or the co-operation of anyone trying to converse with the mentally handicapped person. So for a multiply handicapped client, symbols are the most obvious choice of system, especially in view of the many aids that can help to compensate for his physical difficulties in gaining access to them.

By whatever means a symbol is indicated, its form remains constant and, whether the handicapped person is 'receiving' it or expressing it, only recognition is required of him. He has no need to recall its form for independent production.

Manipulable symbols and in some cases those which appear on a VDU can be scanned, arranged to make up a message, scanned again and re-arranged.

The user has no need to commit himself until he is ready. Either for expression or reception, he can process the symbols at his own speed, even with intermittent lapses of attention, and meanwhile the symbol message remains unchanged. The able receiver of the message does not have to be present while it is being composed, which can be an advantage for, say, a busy teacher with several students to attend to.

On account of their non-transitory nature, symbols can be a very convenient and versatile teaching tool in language development, for labelling of pictures or sets to be sorted, sequencing, pre-reading and reading programmes, and a variety of learning activities. The skill of discriminating non-alphabetic graphic symbols is a foundation for finer distinctions between letters of the alphabet.

Spelled words written on or alongside symbols may familiarise a symbol user with their appearance, though research suggest that transitioning to traditional orthography (TO) is unlikely to take place without specific teaching to that end. The written words will, however, allow a lay person unfamiliar with symbols to read and understand their meaning, which in itself may help to break down barriers between the handicapped person and the rest of the community. If a client's comprehension is wholly dependent on symbols, the lay person can also construct a response – though practice in using the symbols will increase the fluency and naturalness of communication.

In contrast to these advantages, there are a number of disadvantages to the use of symbols, which are perhaps obvious from our earlier discussions.

Most salient is their relative lack of portability. This may be a particularly acute problem when manipulable symbols are involved. Though the use of magnetised symbols can assist to some extent, they can shift into a confused jumble on the carrying tray and are easily dropped and scattered. While certain activities are in progress, movable symbols and even symbol charts become rather impractical; such activities include riding, swimming, using the toilet and to a lesser extent eating and drinking. Some of these activities might otherwise provide especially motivating situations for communication.

Although a user's personality comes over clearly when he is using symbols to good effect, bodily expression is not integral to the system. With symbols, therefore, Total Communication is an ideal more difficult to achieve than in the context of signing. The interaction between user and 'listener' can be less direct. For example, a teacher's attention can be spread among several different pupils, each of whom is engaged in composing a message while waiting his turn for individual attention. Of course this can also be seen as an advantage, an economical way of employing a teacher's limited time, but undeniably it diffuses direct teacher-pupil interaction. The most positive solution, and indeed a way forward, is for pupils to communicate with each other, but this only becomes practicable when pupils have reached a certain level of understanding and motivation.

Extended or more complex communication via a symbol chart requires the internal sequencing of items and so makes the same kind of demands on short-term memory as signing, though at least the symbols are available for scanning before selection. The deterrent to extended expression when using manipulable symbols is that the procedure is time-consuming and somewhat cumbersome, which may lead clients to express less in a less complex manner.

Other Factors in Choosing a System

As learning styles vary, so does the most helpful kind of learning support. All young children need sensorimotor input (i.e. experience gained through the senses) in order to learn and develop. Older mentally handicapped clients, who are still at an early stage of development, can also benefit from the sensorimotor input of signing. If, however, clients are very disturbed or hyperactive, it may be easier to catch and hold their attention with a permanently visible symbol than with a sign; a sign may initially seem to be just one more body movement among so many. Structured pre-training and training help to combat this problem, but certainly the learning steps can be very precisely identified and monitored for success when symbols are involved, whereas 'correct' sign usage may be a matter of judgement.

Even before learning a non-speech system, some clients have well-developed internal language. They then learn to attach expressive labels to the concepts they have already formed. Other clients who lack this internal language are more responsive to concrete cues and are helped by the initial use of real objects, models or miniatures (e.g. a cup or bowl, plaster or plastic food models, or a miniature toilet) in symbol-type programmes. Experience will tell whether an individual learns concept-labels more easily through linkage with the body movement of signing or derives greater support from the visual permanence of symbols. Further teaching would proceed accordingly.

The client's own inclinations may also be a factor in choosing a system, even if he cannot (yet!) communicate them explicitly. He may be more strongly motivated by one or the other.

So Who Should Use What?

Our discussion provides no quick answers to the question of who should use which type of system — and indeed in our experience the most obvious answer is not invariably the 'correct' one. Certain points may, however, indicate the use of one or the other, without in any way allowing watertight diagnoses. These are summarised in Table 6.1.

Uncertainty about a particular client or group may be resolved by introducing a sign system and a symbol system together, so that the possibility exists of each system supporting the other in a kind of symbiotic relationship. In any case, since the options remain open, individual progress and propensities can be monitored against future decisions on the primary communication method.

Table 6.1: Summary of Indicators and Contra-indicators for Use of Sign and Symbol Systems

Indicators of Sign Use	Indicators of Symbol Use
Client uses meaningful gestures	Responds well to pictures
Can/will imitate	Poor short-term memory
Good recall	Poor recall
Wants to learn (and physically able)	Slow to work things out
Readily interacts	Needs very tight structures
	Severely physically handicapped
Contra-indicators of Sign Use	**Contra-indicators of Symbol Use**
Limited motor skills	Poor two-dimensional discrimination
Stereotyped hand movements	Cannot picture-match (but has sign-
Very intermittent attention	relevant abilities)
Frequent changes of carers	

Ultimately, where a client's ability and life-style permit, signing has most to offer in terms of convenience and normalisation, including impetus towards speech. Symbols, however, are extremely practical and appropriate in some circumstances. They can be the best 'way in' to language for especially difficult or low-functioning clients. Their nature is such that technical aids can make them accessible to clients with a severe physical handicap. As a teaching tool, whatever the communicative medium, they form a valuable additional resource. Moreover, just as the use of the written word is an important adjunct to speech, complementing and certainly not replacing it, so a symbol system can serve a parallel function in conjunction with signing.

Authorities and establishments are wise to encourage personnel to obtain a wide knowledge of the various non-speech alternatives, since much can be gained from an eclectic approach. Even if as a general policy one system is adopted, many of the ideas promoted by other approaches can aid communication development. Naturally a detailed knowledge of clients and their needs is equally important.

Setting and Socialisation

Individually based non-speech teaching programmes are more common than programmes orientated to groups. This may seem to contradict the essentially social nature of communication.

Some years ago the professional identity of the person who was developing sign or symbol programmes biased the choice of setting in a particular direction. The majority of studies by research psychologists focused on one individual or a series of individuals. Speech therapy tuition was traditionally conducted one to one, following programmes tailored to suit the individual. In contrast, although withdrawal of individuals has long been an accepted part of remedial education, it was generally felt within the teaching profession that a teacher 'should' be able to manage a group. In special schools too this attitude often prevailed, further influenced by the practical consideration of occupying the rest of the class during a session of individual tuition.

Nowadays attitudes appear to have softened, except perhaps in the research field (as discussed later in this chapter). While many speech therapists have come to believe in the value of group work, teachers of severely mentally handicapped people are well aware that working one to one may be essential with difficult students. Other students may also benefit from withdrawal for some specific language programmes, by escaping from the abundance of non-linguistic cues in the real-life environment. For example, a child may respond appropriately to instructions without attending to the language used, simply by acting in accordance with the context (e.g. 'Put the book ON the table'). A controlled teaching situation can establish whether a concept is really understood (e.g. whether the child understands the distinction between ON, UNDER and IN). The problem of what to do with the rest of a group while one member is being taught is ameliorated when a second adult is available. This is often possible in special schools and may sometimes be so in establishments catering for severely handicapped older groups. The assistant can then supervise the majority during the tuition of an individual.

An advantage of groups, even small ones, is that they are less costly in terms of the personnel required; in addition they can provide extra social motivation for learning. One headteacher suggests that intensity may also help and quotes her school's 'ridiculous sessions with two staff and three children [that] have yielded communication from some who have been unmotivated for years'. In these sessions, humour deriving from 'inappropriate' teacher behaviour seemed to be the trigger for communication.

The group can be a good environment for encouraging conversation and interaction, giving practice for a more general use of practical communication in a wider community. For those who have difficulty in generalising their language outside teaching sessions, structured interaction with peers can help to narrow the gap between the artificially-set-up teaching situation and real life. The ground is then prepared for parents whose mentally handicapped children live at home to help generalise and stimulate 'real' conversation, and carers in a residential setting can also help their charges to appreciate the possibilities offered by communication in the course of daily living.

Some clients thrive on group instruction, their own learning being reinforced by the teaching of others. Once clients can respond even minimally to their peers they are in a position to enjoy and profit from shared teaching experiences in the group. Owing to the nature and severity of their needs, many mentally handicapped people only have demands placed upon them as individuals by individuals. Perhaps they are too often denied the group requirement to conform or, more positively, to prove their own worth.

Research and Development

As an introduction to the topic, this book has limited the number of references to specific examples of research into signs and symbols for mentally handicapped people. In fact, however, much of the published research does not deal with issues that are of great concern to practitioners. Teaching is a complex art and scientists have difficulty in adequately controlling or gauging many of the variables in an everyday eductional context. By the same token, however, if small elements are tidily studied in isolation, the overall validity of their function in a complex teaching environment may be questioned.

Investigating non-speech communication poses special problems for the educational researcher. Signs are not always capable of precise definition; a further difficulty arises when they are used for communication, for their non-verbal context and the manner of their production can attract additional meaning. A straight comparison of systems is problematic because of their differing content (some very extensive, some intentionally restricted) and rationale. Since the systems represent quite distinct philosophies, analysis and comparison of their component parts does not give a true picture of their total worth.

Another difficulty for researchers is that most practitioners are committed to one particular system and lack an equivalent knowledge of competing systems. Professional jealousy may well be involved and thus objectivity in studying relevant issues diminished. As a result, setting up comparative studies of the systems in day-to-day use is no easy task.

A factor which has affected the use made of academic research, particularly in the UK, is that whereas much educational innovation derives from respected academic sources, proponents of non-speech systems have initially been grassroots practitioners. Because of their own practical background, they are sceptical of academics whose skills lie in research rather than practice. Though the academics' basis of knowledge is no less than in relation to other topics they have studied, they have been chided because – not surprisingly – their efficiency in a particular signing system is below the standard of professionals actually working with it.

The nature of research has been affected too because the rise in currency of non-speech systems has coincided with a diminution in funding for educational research. This drop in resources may be one reason why university academics have not spearheaded the innovatory movement. Certainly it has affected the style of research and development. As outlined by Kiernan, Reid and Jones (1982), most of the studies are quite small and limited in their generalisation. Greater available resources might have enhanced the scale and rigour of research.

The Way Forward

Whatever differences of opinion exist over alternative communication systems and approaches to their teaching and use, the needs of a non-speaking mentally handicapped population remain. Even while many issues are as yet unresearched or unproven, practitioners want to offer the best possible deal to their clients. Crusades on behalf of (or against) one system or another are not unknown, but at the present time flexibility and practicality are more in order. It is an admirable philosophy that seems to prevail among engineers and inventors who are concerned with very direct problems, that if an existing device is superseded by something more up to date, then this is accepted as the price of progress. Of course the process of obsolescence of mechanical or electronic devices may be clearer than when abstract ideas are involved.

Regarding practical needs, in the context of issues raised in this book, we see research in the following topics as being particularly relevant:

(1) the diagnostic assessment of clients for various schemes of non-speech intervention;

(2) the effectiveness of different teaching approaches, including single-system learning as compared with joint sign-symbol programmes;

(3) methods of structuring group learning and the effect of different settings on learning and use of systems;

(4) the linguistic function of non-speech systems and their differential effect on speech development;

(5) methods of broadening the knowledge and acceptance of non-speech systems and, allied to this, the role of social and political forces in determining the development of non-speech alternatives.

Pioneering work with non-speech systems and mentally handicapped people has borne exciting results. We must hope that with future developments the thrust will continue, to extend to those who lack it the enabling power of communication.

APPENDIX A: ANNOTATED LIST OF FURTHER READING

Blissymbolics Communication Institute. *A Manner of Speaking*. Blissymbolics Communication Institute, Toronto. Available from Living and Learning, Wisbech, UK. A short free introductory booklet which from a Canadian perspective describes briefly the development and use of Blissymbolics.

Buckley, S. (1985). 'Attaining basic education skills: Reading, writing and number'. In D. Lane and B. Stratford (eds) *Current Approaches to Down's Syndrome*. Holt, Reinhart and Winston, London. A review of relevant research on Down's Syndrome and basic literacy development.

Carlson, F. (1981). *Alternative Methods of Communication: A Handbook for Students and Clinicians*. The Interstate Printers and Publishers, Danville, Illinois. This is a well-illustrated but low-budget book that is rather difficult to obtain outside the USA. It contains a fairly comprehensive account of the general use of alternative methods of communication, with chapters on: Communication devices; Evaluation; and Intervention. There is, however, not a great deal of discussion on the individual merits of rival systems and the alternatives relate purely to an American context. Also the emphasis of the book is not directed at mentally handicapped clients.

   In one appendix a specific 'system' called PICSYM is noted. This has been conceived by Faith Carlson although details are sparse.

Carrier, J.K. Jr and Peak, T. (1975). *Non-Slip Non-Speech Language Initiation Programmes*.H. & H. Enterprises, Lawrence, Kansas. The package and manual are very expensive. However, although the breadth of content is limited the programmes are helpful examples of detailed structured language work.

Deich, R.F. and Hodges, P.M. (1977). *Language without Speech*. Souvenir Press, London. This book essentially consists of two sections. The first part reviews the general background to language development, communication disorders, non-speech alternatives and primate language experiments. The final sections of the book are devoted entirely to the use of Premack-type symbol systems. Both the Non-Slip and their own studies are extensively described. Even if it is not appropriate to use plastic symbols with your clients this book like all those in the *Human Horizon* series is good value. As well as providing a useful review of developments up to 1977 the methodology of structured non-speech tuition is well described.

Gallender, D. (1980). *Symbol Communication for the Severely Handicapped (Sign Language for Classroom Programming and Management)* Charles C. Thomas, Springfield, Illinois. This book consists largely of a vocabulary of American Sign Language (ASL). The elements are well described:

however, in terms of its ASL basis and the restricted concept of language programming, the book may be of limited application in many contexts.

Gorman, P. and Paget, Lady G. (1976). *The Paget Gorman Sign System*. Association for Experiment in Deaf Education, London. The complete vocabulary reference book and manual for the Paget Gorman Sign System (PGSS). Hardly a bed-time read but essential for any professional wishing to implement the PGSS in any setting.

Hehner, Barbara (ed.) (1979). *Blissymbols for Use*. Blissymbolics Communication Institute, Toronto. Available from Living and Learning, Wisbech, UK. The basic source book for those professionals who need a complete reference vocabulary for working with handicapped clients.

Kiernan, C.C., Reid, B.D. and Jones, L.M. (1982). *Signs and Symbols: A Review of Literature and Survey of the Use of Non-Vocal Communication Systems. Studies in Education* No. 11. Institute of Education, University of London. This book's content is largely as described in the title. It is based on research and usage within the UK and therefore reflects the specifically UK development of alternatives to speech for handicapped children (including the mentally handicapped). The style is clear and readable but it is not the aim of the book to be a specific guide to practice.

Latham, C. (1980). *Communication Systems*. Groves Medical Audiovisual Library, Chelmsford. A very slim but clearly explained outline of all the major non-speech alternatives used within the UK. An ideal short introduction to the communication possibilities available to the handicapped but it contains no element of critical comment.

Leeming, K., Swann, W., Coupe, J. and Mittler, P. (1979). *Teaching Language and Communication to the Mentally Handicapped*. Schools Council Bulletin 8. Evans/Methuen Educational, London. Although not centred on sign or symbol alternatives this book contains a seminal report on both theory and practice for teaching language and communication to mentally disabled people. As well as reviews of a variety of approaches specific case studies cast light on the nitty-gritty of teaching and curriculum development.

Living and Learning. *Happy Talking*. Living and Learning, Wisbech, UK. A free introductory leaflet which gives a brief description of the history and development of the Blissymbol system; areas of application; addresses and references. It also contains a full compendium of books and materials related to Blissymbolics that are available from Living and Learning.

Lloyd, L.L. (ed.) (1976). *Communication Assessment and Intervention Strategies*. University Park Press, Baltimore. This is an American book which now is a little outdated. However, apart from general information on communication difficulties, there are chapters which outline details of Blissymbols, Peabody Rebus, Non-SLIP signing systems and communication aids. Not really a book for an individual to buy but still an excellent reference and source of information.

McDonald, E.J. (1980). *Teaching and Using Blissymbols*. Blissymbolics Communication Institute, Toronto. Available from Living and Learning, Wisbech, UK. A straightforward book which focuses on the system of Blissymbolics, assessment, programme development, implementation and the various ways of accessing symbols.

McNaughton, S., Kates, B. and Silverman, H. (1978). *Handbook of Blissymbolics*. Blissymbolics Communication Institute, Toronto. Available from Living and Learning, Wisbech, UK. A large loose-leaf bound compendium written for instructors, symbol users, parents and administrators. The handbook contains the following sections: The Blissymbol System; Physical Functional Considerations; Application of the System; and Appendices detailing interface information.

Peter, M. and Barnes, R. (eds) (1982). *Signs, Symbols and Schools: an introduction to the use of Non-Vocal Communication Systems and Sign Language in Schools*. National Council for Special Education, UK. This very useful large booklet contains a compilation of articles previously published in the journal *Special Education: Forward Trends*, covering the wide area of interest of the title, not just the mentally handicapped Each section is written by a key enthusiast for a particular mode of communication. However, the leading sage of alternatives to speech within the UK, Chris Kiernan, has written a carefully balanced leading article.

Schiefelbusch, R.L. (ed.) (1980). *Non-speech Language and Communication: Analysis and Intervention*. University Park Press, Baltimore. This is an excellent comprehensive American book, composed of a number of chapters by experts on specific aspects of non-speech education. There are overall sections related to American Sign Language, assessment of non-speech communication and strategies for autistic and severely retarded children. Perhaps the main feature of this series of contributions is that in many instances the individual authors manage to get beyond the mere presentation of a specific innovation, and there is a refreshing degree of critical discussion relating to both general and specific application, and teaching issues.

Silverman, F.H. (1980). *Communication for the Speechless*. Prentice Hall, Englewood Cliffs, NJ. This book offers a guide to the use of non-speech alternatives in North America only. Obviously this represents a limitation. However, there are extensive details on symbol systems that are used worldwide and a section on communication aids.

There are very useful appendices which include sources for aids and components, however, these are of less interest to professionals working within the UK. Overall the book is more relevant if a UK client's main handicap is physical.

Skelly, M. (1979). *Amer-Ind Gestural Code Based on Universal American Indian Hand Talk*. Elsevier Press, New York. A large clearly written book which can be difficult to obtain in the UK. In many ways this represents the

Amer-Ind bible; research, project details, assessment guidelines, practical use and an extensive vocabulary are very neatly combined in a relatively easy read.

Spastics Society. *The Paget Gorman Sign System: A reference book for parents and teachers* No. 1. The Spastics Society, London. A small well-displayed illustration of a useful basic vocabulary for severely intellectually disabled school children. Perhaps not as precise or expansive as the full Paget Gorman Sign System manual but is easy to use and not at all daunting for those who are less experienced with the system.

Tebbs, J. (co-ordinator) (1978). *Ways and Means*. Globe Education, Basingstoke. Designed as a general resource book for those working with the language-retarded child and modestly compiled by Somerset Education Authority, it contains a wealth of detail and sources of information on non-speech alternatives. A truly pioneering publication, it still is essential reading for any person with a practical interest in the development of signs and symbols for the disabled.

Thatcher, J. (1984). *Teaching Reading to Mentally Handicapped Children*. Croom Helm, London and Canberra. This book in the Croom Helm *Special Education* series represents one of the few practical books which provides an encouraging programme to try to establish basic literacy in as wide a range of mentally handicapped children as possible. A variety of strategies are presented so that a teacher can choose what is appropriate for the pupils for whom they are responsible.

Vanderheiden, G.C. and Grilley, K. (ed.) (1975). *Non-Vocal Communication Techniques and Aids for the Severely Physically Handicapped*. University Park Press, Baltimore. Based upon transcriptions of the 1975 Trace Center National Workshop Series on non-vocal communication techniques and aids, this large book is less topical now. As the title suggests, the content is directed to symbols and their application to the physically handicapped. There is, however, a chapter by Deborah Harris-Vanderheiden on an early application of Blissymbols with mentally handicapped children.

Warrick, A. *Blissymbols for Pre-School Children* (1982). Ottawa Crippled Children Treatment Centre. Available from Living and Learning, Wisbech, UK. This booklet was written by an experienced speech pathologist. It contains information on assessment, initiating a programme, appropriate vocabulary and the creative use of Blissymbols. Teaching children who are developing receptive as well as expressive language is of obvious application to intellectually disabled individuals.

APPENDIX B: SOURCES OF FURTHER INFORMATION

ACE (Aids to Communication in Education Centre)
Prue Fuller, Ormorod School, Wayneflete Road, Headington, Oxford OX3 8DD. Telephone: Oxford (0865) 635508.

Amer-Ind
Semed Inc., 36100 Genesee Lake Road, Oconomawoe, Wisconsin, USA
Suzanne Leavesley, 7 Chester Close, Lichfield, Staffordshire, UK. Office telephone: Stafford (0785) 56231.

Blissymbolics
Blissymbolics Communicaton Institute, 350 Rumsey Road, Toronto, Canada M4G 1R8. Telephone: (416) 425 7835.
Blissymbolics Communication Resource Centre (UK), South Glamorgan Institute of Higher Education, Western Avenue, Llandaff, Cardiff CF5 2YB. Telephone: Cardiff (0222) 551770.
Living and Learning, Duke Street, Wisbech, Cambridgeshire PE13 2AE. Telephone: Wisbech (0945) 63441. As well as publishing a great deal of general language development materials relevant to non-speech alternatives, Living and Learning act as agents in the UK for publications officially promoted by the Canadian Centre of the International Blissymbolics Institute.

BSL Research Workshop
Jim Kyle, Sign Language Project, School of Education Research Unit, Bristol University, 19 Berkeley Square, Bristol BS8 1HS. A unit devoted to the linguistic analysis of British Sign Language (BSL), therefore information is generally of background interest to those working with non-speech alternatives for the mentally disabled.

BSL Makaton Vocabulary
Makaton Vocabulary Development Project, 31 Firwood Drive, Camberley, Surrey. Telephone: Camberley (0276) 61390. This is the central address for any information or material related to the Makaton Vocabulary.

Communication Aid Centres (England and Wales)
Six centres have recently been established by the DHSS with funding from the Royal Association for Disability and Rehabilitation (RADAR) and the Department of Trade and Industry (DOTI) to provide advice on communication aids, their use and acquisition.

At the present time centres are sited rather inconveniently to give national coverage. However, the innovation of providing these units is a real plus in terms of the appropriate application of communication aids.

Centres and Contacts

Julia Le Patourel
Communication Aids Centre
Charing Cross Hospital
Fulham Palace Road
London W6
Tel.: 01 748 2040

Eileen Burke
Communication Aids Centre
Roakwood Hospital
Fairwater Road
Llandaff
Cardiff
Tel.: 0222 566281

Liz Panton/Philip Lowe
Communication Aids Centre
Castle Farm Road
Newcastle Upon Tyne
Tel.: 091-284 0480

Nicola Jolleff
Communication Aids Centre
The Wolfson Centre
Mecklenburgh Square
London WC1N 2AP
Tel.: 01 837 7618 and
01 278 4902

Jayne Easton/Jane Bennett
Communication Aids Centre
Frenchay Hospital
Bristol BS16 1LE
Tel.: 0272 565656

Kathryn Robinson/Clive Thursfield
Communication Aids Centre
Boulton Road
West Bromwich
Birmingham
Tel.: 021 553 0908

Kiernan, Chris
Director, Hester Adrian Research Centre, The University, Manchester M13 9PL. Telephone: 061 273 3333. Chris Kiernan and his associates, previously at the Thomas Coram Unit, London, have represented the major source of independent practical research into the use of non-speech alternatives within the UK.

Lloyd, Lyle L.
Professor and Chairman of Special Education and Professor of Audiology and Speech Sciences, Purdue University, South Campus Courts – E, Indiana 47907. Telephone: (317) 494 7330. One of the leading researchers and reviewers of non-speech alternatives in the USA. Many of his doctoral students have added many interesting studies in this area of concern.

Non-SLIP
H. & H. Enterprises, Box 3342, Lawrence, Kansas 66044, USA. The sole source for any information on Non-SLIP. Very obligingly they will usually send free quite an extensive package of information. However, the Non-SLIP materials themselves are rather expensive.

Paget-Gorman Sign System (Paget Gorman Signed Speech)
Bob Newey, 106 Morrell Avenue, Oxford OX4 1NA.

Rebus Peabody Rebus
Ken Jones, Bristol Polytechnic, Bristol.
Judy van Oosterom, c/o Living and Learning, Duke Street, Wisbech, UK. Telephone: 0945 63441. A vital contact for any professional wishing to set

up a comprehensive communication scheme, especially if one is interested specifically in Rebus-related techniques.

American Guidance Service Inc., Publishers Building, Circle Pines, Minnesota 55014, USA. The official publishers for standard non-adapted Peabody Rebus materials.

Educational Evaluation Enterprises, Awre, Newnham, Gloucestershire GL14 1ET. Telephone: (059) 451 503. The main supplier of official Peabody Rebus books and materials in the UK. A free catalogue is available on request.

Remington, Bob and Light, Paul

The Department of Psychology, University of Southampton, SO9 5HN, Hampshire. Telephone: Southampton (0703) 559122. Within the UK there has been relatively little adequately conducted academic research into non-speech alternatives for the handicapped. Although their work mainly with plastic symbol tuition for severely retarded non-speaking children may seem a little esoteric to those concerned with practical issues, they have a fund of knowledge on the caution that is required in interpreting over-enthusiastic research findings.

SEMERCs (Special Education Micro Electronics Resource Centres)

Co-ordinated by the Microelectronics and Education Programme (MEP) Special Education Project, these centres play a vital role in the UK in both displaying and disseminating information relating to both software and hardware and their application to special education. The newsletter updates the rapid changes in this area.

National Co-ordinator
Mary Hope
Council for Educational Technology
Devonshire Street
London W1N 2BA
Tel.: 01 580 7553

Bristol SEMERC
Jean Johnstone (Manager)
Faculty of Education
Bristol Polytechnic
Redland Hill
Bristol BS6 6UZ
Tel.: 0272 733141

Redbridge SEMERC
Andrew Fluck (Manager)
Dane Centre
Melbourne Road
Ilford, Essex IG1 4HZ
Tel.: 01 478 6363

Newcastle SEMERC
Colin Richards (Manager)
Newcastle Polytechnic
Coach Lane Campus
Newcastle Upon Tyne NE7 7XA
Tel.: 0912 665057

Manchester SEMERC
Bob Dyke (Manager)
Manchester Polytechnic
Hathersage Road
Manchester Road
Manchester M13 0JA
Tel.: 061 225 9054

Signed English

Karen Saulnier, Research Associate, The Signed English Project, The Gallaudet Research Institute, Center for Studies in Education and Human Development, Gallaudet College, Washington DC 20002, USA. Gallaudet College is one of the major centres in the USA for the development of signing and sign language.

D.J. Sayer, Research and Information Officer, Working Party on Signed English, 12 Deepdene Gardens, Dorking, Surrey RH4 2BH, UK. Telephone: Dorking (0306) 882065. Previously very little information on Signed English in the UK was available in print. However, the Working Party has recently published a book *Signed English for Schools*, Volume I.

B.S. Armstrong, Chairman, Working Party on Signed English, Royal School for Deaf Children, Victora Road, Margate, Kent CT9 1NB, UK. Telephone: Margate (0843) 27561. This institution together with a few other special schools in the south of England has revitalised interest in Signed English (SE) in the UK and has the most extensive experience of the practical development of SE with deaf school children.

Sigsymbols

Ailsa Cregan, Home: 76 Wood Close, Hatfield, AL10 8TX. Telephone: 070 72 64587. Office: Coles Green School, Dollis Hill Lane, London NW2. Telephone: 01 450 2550. One of the authors of this book and the deviser and developer of Sigsymbols.

Traditional Alphabetic Script

Mrs Sue Buckley, Senior Lecturer, Department of Psychology, Portsmouth Polytechnic, King Charles Street, Portsmouth. Telephone: (0705) 738606 ext. 370 or 368. Sue Buckley has promoted both research and development into encouraging literacy in pre-school Down's children in combination with either speech or sign. She uses primarily a whole word method and as well as being able to give workshops, pamphlets or videos are available and a full review of related relevant research is to be found in Buckley (1985) (see Bibliography).

Worldsign

Worldsign Communication Society, Perry Siding, Winlow, BC, Canada VO6 2JO. Telephone: (604) 355 2408. David Orcutt at this address is the major source worldwide for a sign/symbol system which as yet has not been developed for use with people who have learning difficulties.

APPENDIX C: SUPPLIERS OF COMMUNICATION AIDS – A SELECTION

Canon (UK) Ltd

Airport House, Purley Way, Croydon CR0 0XZ. Telephone: 01 680 8880. Produce the Canon Communicator. Designed for children and adults with speech disorders. Not very relevant for people with fine motor or severe learning disabilities as a small alphabetic keyboard is displayed.

Carba Ltd

Waldeggstrasse, 38 CH-3097 Libefeld-Bern, Switzerland. The company produces indicators and was one of the first companies to use a computer-based communication system for handicapped people.

Chailey Heritage

Rehabilitation Engineering Unit, Chailey Heritage, Lewes, East Sussex. As well as general aids, Chailey produces a series of robust communication items like head pointers, chart holders, switches and light displays.

Convaid

The Avenue, Eastbourne, East Sussex BR21 3YA. This company produces an electronic speaking aid operated via a flat 64-square keyboard. By pressing selected keys in sequence a sentence can be produced. Each element is stored in the unit's memory and released as a full spoken phrase when required by pressing a SPEAK key. The word bank can be varied and the visual cues changed via transparent overlays.

Dufco

901 Iva Court, Cambria, California 93428, USA. Produces a 10×10 matrix selector with memory for eight positions and changeable overlay sheets. Interface switches can be supplied.

Magpie Systems

J.N. Tabberer, 51 Guernsey Close, Widnes WA8 0YH. Produces Micro-mike, a modified CB microphone, which may be plugged directly into the analogue input on the back of a BBC Model B microcomputer. The Micromike gives a simple voice switching control and plays back input.

Phonic Ear Ltd (Canada)

747 Kimbel Street, Unit 10, Minissauga, Ontario L5S 1E7, Canada. Telephone: 416 677 3231. Telex: 06-968754.

Phonic Ear Inc. (USA)

250 Camino Alto, Mill Valley, CA 94941, USA. Telephone: 415 383 4000.

Possum Controls Limited

Middlegreen Road, Langley, Slough, Berkshire SL3 6DF. Fifteen years ago Possum was the only company in the UK which produced electronic communication aids on any scale. In recent years, the whole technological world has changed, making some Possum items rather dated, though the company is now marketing a whole range of newly developed items.

QED (Quest Educational Designs)
1 Prince Alfred Street, Gosport, Hampshire PO12 1QH. This company markets visuo-motor scanners, rotary pointer boards and a range of input switches. Although more sophisticated electronic items have been developed, the company still produces a range of the more basic electro-mechanical devices.

Queenswood Scientific
1 The Paddock, Stubbington, Fareham, Hampshire PO14 3NS. Telephone: Stubbington (03295) 61993. Queenswood's products are unusual in that most items are not directly practical aids but rather training equipment designed specifically to attract children, e.g. reward toys and gaze communicators.

Telemachus Ltd
PO Box 86, Aylesbury, Buckinghamshire. As well as indicator boards and rotary pointers, Telemachus produces items to encourage children to point. A touch-sensitive organ is a particularly stimulating item.

Tools for Living
PO Box 13, Godalming, Surrey GU7 1TA. This company can provide activator switches.

VA Howe-Co Ltd
12-14 St Ann's Crescent, London SW18 2LS. This company can provide activator switches.

Western Information Technological Services Ltd
49 Dial Hill Road, Clevedon, Avon BS21 7EW. This firm produces a practical very portable voice synthesiser operated via a flat simplified keyboard which is capable of accepting a range of symbol inputs.

Weyfringe Limited
Langbeck Road, Marske, Redcar, Cleveland TS11 6HQ. Telephone: (0642) 470121. Weyfringe has a range of devices with a visual memory. Unfortunately it relies completely on a conventional alphabet and therefore is of minor relevance to most mentally handicapped people.

Zygo Industries
Box 1008, 3102 South West 87, Portland, Oregon 97225, USA. Zygo markets display boards and battery-powered portable indicators.

BIBLIOGRAPHY

Bailey, P.A. (in prep.). *Introducing Blissymbols*. Blissymbolics Communication Institute, Toronto.

Bailey, R.D. (1978). 'Makaton Success: Fact and Artefact', *Apex*, **6**(3), 18–19.

Bleck, E. and Nagel, D. (1982). *Physically Handicapped Children: A Medical Atlas for Teachers (2nd ed.)*. Grune and Stratton, New York.

Bliss, C. (1965). *Semantography*. Semantography Publications Sydney, Australia.

Blissymbolics Communication Institute (1985). *The Blissymbolics Independent Study Program*. Blissymbolics Communication Institute, Toronto.

Blissymbolics Communication Institute (1985). *Picture Your Blissymbols*. Blissymbolics Communication Institute, Toronto.

Blissymbolics Communication Institute (1985). *The Synrell Programmes*. Blyssymbolics Communication Institute, Toronto.

Bloom, L. and Lahey, M. (1978). *Language Development and Language Disorders*. Wiley, New York.

Boehm, A.E. (1971). *Boehm Test of Basic Concepts*. The Psychological Corporation, New York.

Bornstein, H., Saulnier, K.L. and Hamilton, L.B. (1983). *The Comprehensive Signed English Dictionary*. Gallaudet College Press, Kendal Green, Washington.

Bricker, D.D.(1972). 'Imitative Sign Training as a Facilitator of Word Association with Low Functioning Children', *American Journal of Mental Deficiency*, **76**(1), 509–160.

Bricker, W.A. and Bricker, D.D. (1970). 'A Programme of Language Training for the Severely Handicapped Child', *Exceptional Child*, **37**(2), 101–11.

Brown, R. (1973). *A First Language: The Early Stages*. MIT Press, Cambridge, Mass. (or 1976, Penguin Books Ltd. Harmondsworth).

Bryant, P. (1974). *Perception and Understanding in Young Children: an Experimental Approach*. Methuen, London.

Buckley, S. (1984). *Reading and Language Development in Children with Down's Syndrome*. Portsmouth Polytechnic, Portsmouth.

Buckley, S. (1985). 'Attaining Basic Education Skills: Reading, Writing and Number' In D. Lane and B. Stratford (eds) *Current Approaches to Down's Syndrome*. Holt, Reinhart and Winston, London.

Butterfield, E.C., Wambold, C. and Belmont, J.M. (1973). 'On the Theory and Practice of Improving Short Term Memory.' *American Journal of Mental Deficiency*, 77, 654–59.

Byler, J.K. (1985). 'The Mahleton Vocabulary'. An Analysis based on Recent Research', *British Journal of Special Education*, **12**(3),pp. 113–20, research supplement.

Carrier, J.K. and Peak, T. (1975). *Non-Speech Language Initiation Program*. H. & H. Enterprises, Lawrence, Kansas.

Carron, E. (1973). *Test for Auditory Comprehension of Language*. Teaching Resources Corporation, New York.

Clark, C.R. (1981). 'Learning Words Using Traditional Orthography and the Symbols of Rebus, Bliss and Carrier', *Journal of Speech and Hearing Disorders*, **46**(2), 191–6.

Clark, C.R. and Greco, J.A. (1973). *MELDS Glossary of Rebuses and Signs*. Research, Development and Demonstration Center in Education of Handicapped Children, University of Minnesota, Minneapolis.

Clark, C.R. and Moores, D.F. (1984). *Clark Early Language Program*. DLM Teaching Resources, Allen, Texas.

Clark, C.R., Davies, C.O. and Woodcock, R.W. (1974). *Standard Rebus Glossary*. American Guidance Service, Circle Pines, Minnesota.

Clark, C.R. Moores, D.F. and Woodcock, R.W. (1975). *The Minnesota Early Language Development Sequence*. Research, Development and Demonstration Center in Education of Handicapped Children, University of Minnesota, Minneapolis.

Cornell, K. (1984). 'BBC Computer Bliss Program: Schools Computer Development Centre, Nottingham', *Blissymbolics Communication Institute: British Newsletter*, July No. 15, 6–7.

Craig, E. (1978). 'Introducing the Paget Gorman Sign System'. In T. Tebbs (ed.) *Ways and*

Means. Globe Education, Basingstoke. Pp. 162–3.

Creedon, M. (1976). *'The David School: A Simultaneous Communication Model'*. Paper presented at the National Society for Autistic Children Meeting, Oak Brook, Illinois. (Available from the author at the Dysfunctioning Child Center, Michael Reese Medical Center, Chicago, Illinois 60616.)

Cregan, A. (1980). *'Sigsymbols — A Non-Vocal Aid to Communication and Language Development'*. Unpublished long study, Cambridge Institute of Education.

Cregan, A. (1982). Sigsymbol Dictionary/Teaching Pack. Published by the author, 76 Wood Close, Hatfield, Herts.

Crystal, D. (1979). *Working with LARSP: Studies in Language Disability and Remediation*. Arnold, London.

Crystal, D., Fletcher, P. and Garman, M. (1976). *The Grammatical Analysis of Language Disability: A Procedure for Assessment and Remediation*. Arnold, London.

Cunningham, C. (1982). *Down's Syndrome: An Introduction for Parents*. Souvenir Press, London.

Daniloff, J. and Shafer, A. (1981). 'A Gestural Programme for Severely-Profoundly Handicapped Children.' *Language of Speech and Hearing Services in the Schools*, **12**, 258–67.

Deich, R.F. and Hodges, P.M. (1977). *Language Without Speech*. Souvenir Press, London.

Derrick, J. (1977). *The Child's Acquisition of Language*. NFER, Slough.

Devereux, K. and van Oosterom, J. (1984). *Learning with Rebuses*. NCSE, Stratford Upon Avon.

Dunn, M., Leota, M., Whettan, C. and Pintillie, D. (1982). *The British Picture Vocabulary Test*. NFER — Nelson Publishing Company, Windsor.

Fenn, G. (1976). 'Against Verbal Enrichment'. In P. Berry (ed.) *Language and Communication in the Mentally Handicapped*. Arnold, London.

Fenn, G. and Rowe, J.A. (1975). 'An Experiment in Manual Communication'. *British Journal of Disorders of Communication*, **10**(1), 3–16.

Finnie, N. (1974). *Handling the Young Cerebral Palsied Child at Home*. Heinemann Medical Books, London.

Fristoe, M. and Lloyd, L.L. (1979). 'Nonspeech Communication'. In N.R. Ellis (ed.) *Handbook of Mental Deficiency*, (2nd. ed.). Lawrence Erlbank Associates, Hilldale, N.J.

Fristoe, M. and Lloyd, L.L. (1980). 'Planning an Initial Expressive Sign Lexicon for Persons with Severe Communication Impairment', *Journal of Speech and Hearing Disorders*, **45**(2), 170–80.

Furneaux, B. and Roberts, B. (1977). *Autistic Children: Teaching, Community and Research Approaches*. Routledge and Kegan Paul, London.

Gardner, R.A. and Gardner, B.T. (1969). 'Teaching Sign Language to a Chimpanzee,' *Science*, **165**(3894), 664–72.

Gersten, R.M. (1980).'In Search of the Cognitive Deficit in Autism: Beyond the Stimulus Overselectivity Model', *Journal of Special Education*, **14**(1), 47–65.

Gillham, B. (1979). *The First Words Language Programme*. Allen and Unwin, London.

Gillham, B. (1983). *Two Words Together: A First Sentences Language Programme*. Allen and Unwin, London.

Gillham, B. (1986). (ed.) *Handicapping Conditions in Children*. Croom Helm, Beckenham.

Grossman, D.H. (n.d.). *A Guide for Parents of Very Young Deaf Children*. Deaf Children's Society, London.

Hehner, B. (1980). *Blissymbols for Use*. Blissymbolics Communication Institute, Toronto, Canada.

Hind, M. (1985). *The Synrell Programmes, 1, 2 and 4*. Distributed by the author: Head of Computer Education, Edge Hill College of Higher Education, St. Helen's Road, Ormskirk, Lancs., U.K.

Hobson, P.A. and Duncan, P. (1979). 'Sign Learning and Profoundly Retarded People', *Mental Retardation*, **17**(1) 33–7.

Hogg, B. (1984). *Microcomputers and Special Educational Needs: A Guide to Good Practice. Developing Horizons in Special Education*, National Council for Special Education, No. 5, Stratford Upon Avon.

House, N.J., Hanley, M.J. and Magid, D.F. (1980). 'Logographic Reading by TMR Adults,' *American Journal of Mental Deficiency*, **82**(2), 161–70.

Jay Report (1979). *Report of the Committee of Enquiry into Mental Handicap Nursing and Care*. HMSO, London.

Jeffree, D. and Skeffington, M. (1980). *Let Me Read*. Souvenir Press, London.

Jones, K. (1978). 'Peabody Rebus Reading Scheme.' In T. Tebbs (ed.) *Ways and Means*. Globe Education, Basingstoke.

Jones, K. (1979). 'A Rebus System of Non-fade Visual Language', *Child: care, health and development*, **5**(1), 1–7.

Jones, P.,R. (1983). ' "Symbol Accentuation": a Controlled Comparison of its Effectiveness for Teaching Initial Word Recognition to Mentally Handicaped Pupils.' *BPS Division of Educational and Child Psychology Occasional Papers*, **7**(1), 24–30.

Karlan, G.R. and Lloyd, L.L. (1983). 'Considerations in the Planning of Communication Intervention: II. Manual Sign and Gestural Systems for Representing the Lexicon', *Journal of the Association for the Severely Handicapped*, **8**, 13–25.

Keller, H. (1966). *The Story of My Life*. Hodder, London.

Kiernan, C.C. (1977). '*A Note on the Derivation of the Revised Makaton Vocabulary*'. Unpublished manuscript.

Kiernan, C.C., Jordan, R.R. and Saunders, C.A. (1978). *Starting Off*. Souvenir Press, London.

Kiernan, C., Reid, B. and Jones, L. (1982). *Signs and Symbols: Use of Non-Vocal Communication Systems*. Heinemann Educational Books, London.

Kirman, B. and Bicknell, J. (1975). (eds) *Mental Handicap*. (Churchill) Livingstone, London.

Knowles, W. and Masidlouer, M. (1979). *Derbyshire Language Scheme Teaching Manual*. Private publication, Ripley, Derbyshire.

Kolvin, I. and Fundudis, T. (1981). 'Electively Mute Children: Psychological Development and Background Factors', *J. of Child Psychology and Psychiatry*, **22**, 219–32.

Kopchick, G.A. Jr and Lloyd, L.L. (1976). 'Total Communication Programming for the Severely Language Impaired: A 24 Hour Approach.' In L.L. Lloyd (ed.) *Communication Assessment and Intervention Strategies*. University Park Press, Baltimore.

Kotkin, R.A., Simpson, S.B. and Desanto, D. (1978). 'The Effect of Sign Language in Picture Norming in Two Retarded Girls Possessing Normal Hearing', *Journal of Mental Deficiency Research*, **22**, 19–25.

Kyle, J. (1982). 'Signs of Speech: Co-operating in Deaf Education.' In M. Peter and R. Barnes, *Signs, Symbols and Schools: an Introduction to the Use of Non-vocal Communication Systems and Sign Language in Schools*. Pp. 25–32.

Kyle, J., Woll, B. and Deuchar, M. (1981). (eds.) *Perspectives on British Sign Language and Deafness*. Croom Helm, Beckenham.

Kyle, J.G., Woll, B., and Llewellyn-Jones, P. (1981). 'Learning and Using BSL', *Sign Language Studies*, **31**, 155–78.

Lane, D. and Stratford, B. (1985). *Current Approaches to Down's Syndrome*. Holt, Reinhart and Winston, London.

Levitt, S. (1979). *Treatment of Cerebral Palsy and Motor Delay*. Blackwell Scientific Publications, Oxford.

Lloyd, L.L. and Daniloff, J. (1983). 'Issues in Using Amer-Ind Code with Retarded Persons.' In T.M. Gallacher and C.A. Prutting (eds.) *Pragmatic Assessment and Intervention Issues in Language*. College Hill Press, San Diego, California.

McDonald, E.T. (1980). *Teaching and Using Blissymbolics*. Blissymbolics Communication Institute, Toronto.

Mein, R. and O'Connor, N. (1960). 'A Study of the Oral Vocabularies of Severely Subnormal Patients.' *Journal of Mental Deficiency Research*, **4**, 130–47.

Miller, A. (1968). *Symbol Accentuation — A New Approach to Reading*. Doubleday Multimedia, Santa Ana, California.

Murphy, G.H., Steele, K., Gilligan, T., Yeow, J. and Spare, D. (1977). 'Teaching a Picture Language to a Non-Speaking Retarded Boy', *Behaviour Research and Therapy*, **15**, 198–201.

Newson, E. and Hipgrave, T. (1982). *Getting Through to your Handicapped Child: A Handbook for Parents, Foster-Parents Teachers and Anyone Caring for Handicapped Children*. Cambridge University Press.

Nolan, M. and Tucker, I.G. (1981). *The Hearing-Impaired Child and the Family*. Souvenir Press, London.

Orcutt, D. (1983). *Worldsign Examples*. Worldsign Communication Society, Perry Siding, BC, Canada.

Paget, R., Gorman, P. and Paget, G. (1976). *The Paget Gorman Sign System (6th ed.)*. Association for Experiment in Deaf Education, London.